New Brunswick Sea Stories

Phantom Ships
and Pirate's Gold
Shipwrecks and Iron Men

by Dorothy Dearborn

Illustrations by Ralph Olive

New Brunswick Sea Stories
A paperback original from Neptune Publishing Company Ltd.

1098765432
Copyright © 1998 by Dorothy Dearborn

Canadian Cataloguing in Publication Data
ISBN 1-896270-13-1
Dearborn, Dorothy 1927-

New Brunswick Sea Stories – Phantom Ships and Pirates Gold Shipwrecks and Iron Men

1. Shipwrecks --New Brunswick. 2 Mutiny -- New Bruns-wick 3. Hijacking of ships -- New Brunswick 1. Title

FC2470.85D42 1998   971.5'1   C98–950225–2
F1042.6.D42 1998

Cover Design by Dorothy Dearborn and Ralph Olive
Illustrations by Ralph Olive

Typesetting by Dearborn Group, Hampton, NB

Neptune Publishing Company Ltd.
116 Prince William Street, Box 6941
Saint John, NB E2L 4S4

New Brunswick Sea Stories

Other books by Dorothy Dearborn

Non Fiction
True Stories New Brunswickers at War
Neptune Publishing 1997
*Legends Oddities Mysteries
and UFO experiences in New Brunswick*
Neptune Publishing 1996
New Brunswick's Unsung Heroes
Neptune Publishing 1996
Madness and Murder in New Brunswick
Neptune Publishing 1995
*New Brunswick Ghosts Demons
and things that go bump in the night!*
Neptune Publishing 1994
Unsolved New Brunswick Murders
Neptune Publishing 1993

Biographies
Dyslexia Dr. Arthur Chesley, Saint John
Dearborn Group 1992
Give Me Fifteen Minutes Roy Alward of Havelock
Unipress Limited, Fredericton 1978

Collections
*Partners in Progress, New Brunswick
Atlantic Canada–At the Dawn of a New Nation*
Windsor Publications Ltd. Burlington, Ontario, 1990

Anthologies
Willie, a short story
Stubborn Strength, A New Brunswick Anthology
Michael O. Nowlan, Academic Press Canada, 1983

Young Adult
The Secret of Pettingill Farms,
Avalon Books, New York 1972
The Mystery of Wood Island,
Avalon Books, New York 1973

New Brunswick Sea Stories

Sea Fever

I must go down to the sea again
To the lonely sea and the sky
And all I ask is a tall ship
And a star to steer her by
by John Masefield
1878-1967
Named Poet Laureate
of England 1930

Contents

Contents

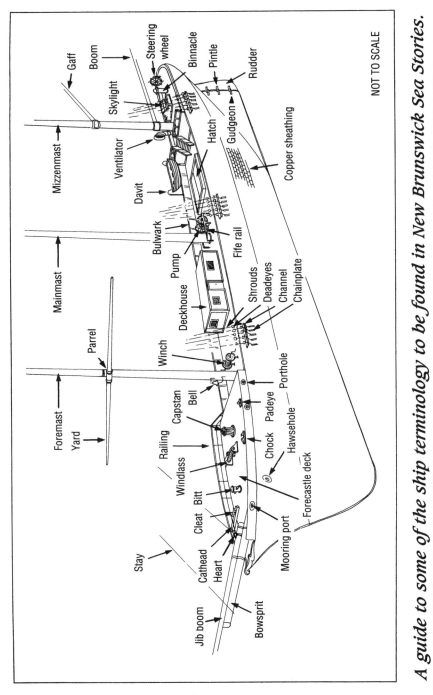

A guide to some of the ship terminology to be found in *New Brunswick Sea Stories.*

NOT TO SCALE

Acknowledgements

There are so many places to go and so many people to see and so many books to read when researching a topic such as the one for this book, Sea Stories of New Brunswick, that it is difficult to know where to start in acknowledging the help I have received along the way.

As always the staff information department of the Saint John Regional Library has proved to be invaluable in the assistance they have provided. Each and every one of these competent young women not only takes an interest in what I am researching but makes a valuable contribution to my work on every occasion. I have come to the conclusion I would be incapable of writing a book without their help. Once again, Thank You.

Fellow writers have also been generous in sharing their knowledge and material with me, most notably A.J. McCarthy of Bathurst who gave me carte blanche to the information in his book and the brain of Harold Adams associate editor of the Miramichi Leader. He is the repository of a gold mine of historical facts of that rich area.

Other writers whose work I have referred to are acknowledged within the stories that contain reference to their work.

While care has been taken to trace the ownership of all copyright material used in the text I, as author, and Neptune Publishing Company Ltd. as publishers welcome any information enabling us to rectify and reference or credit in subsequent editions.

New Brunswick Sea Stories

The Romance of the Sea in the Age of Sail

Whether we were born here in Atlantic Canada or are newcomers to the taste of dulse, the temptation of tiptoeing across red mud flats ... thrilling to the chilling stimulation that only sea water can create ... we succumbed to the romance of sea and sail with our first deep breath of salt sea air.

Love of the sea is as natural as breathing, the sea is our common womb and we weave our tales around it, finding mermaids on rocks, spirits in sails and phantoms everywhere. We love the stories for themselves and for their ability to let us dream of what might have been and, at times, what really was.

When I first made the decision to do this book I didn't realize how far reaching the subject of shipwrecks might be but I quickly learned that it is a far greater project than what might be contained in one small book. Bearing that knowledge in mind I have attempted to put a wide variety of stories in some semblance of order. The result ranges from Phantoms and Sea Monsters to Mayhem and Murder, Iron Men in Wooden Ships and Shipwrecks ... Monuments or Play Toys?

One might say they run the gamut of life. There's even one miracle among them.

St. Martins, family ties and famous ship builders

On April 25, 1938, an obituary in *The Saint John Globe* heralded Frederick M. Cochrane as "one of the most informed men in the Maritime Provinces on the history of ships of the wooden era."

Cochrane operated an accounting and insurance business out of the offices of Saint John sail maker George E. Holder but it was the wooden ships of his childhood in St. Martins, and later in Saint John, that caught his imagination.

That imagination and fascination coupled with a mind meticulous in its attention to detail have resulted in some of the most intriguing sagas of New Brunswick's age of sail to be found anywhere today.

That same obituary noted that, in addition to his "great fund of written knowledge on ships he was noted for his keen memory. It was said he could describe without hesitation facts surrounding the building, command, voyages and eventual end of the career of 500 vessels which slid down the ways at St. Martins, Quaco, Tynemouth Creek and other famous shipyards in the country."

Cochrane also wrote a complete history of ships built in St. John County with general background and data on the shipbuilding industry at that time.

Several of his manuscripts, including information on the whaling fleets of Saint John, were willed at the time of his death to the Saint John Free Public Library where they are carefully preserved in the special archival reference section.

Like writers such as American author Edward Rowe Snow, prolific chronicler of mysteries and legends of the sea, and New Brunswick writer Stuart Trueman I have unabashedly delved into these papers and presented for today's reader some of Cochrane's most fascinating stories.

From what I have read of the man I truly believe he intended his papers to be used by writers so that this colourful account of our past will not be lost to future generations.

In addition I lay some claim to that St. Martins seafaring blood that sailed New Brunswick ships around the world, regularly breaking speed records along the way.

My great-grandfather, Captain William Tufts was one of those men. Until a few years ago I knew little about him save that there was an impressive connection to Tufts University in Boston and that he drowned in Saint John Harbour after falling overboard from his ship! It was this story that led me to his background.

I was visiting in St. Martins one day a few years ago and learned that the Tufts family was in residence at their cottage not far from the Quaco Inn. Seizing the opportunity to learn a bit more about this elusive ancestor I trotted over for a visit.

Mrs. Tufts and I chatted for awhile about this commonality of name and I related the only story I knew, that of my great-grandfather having fallen overboard and drowned in Saint John Harbour.

"How can that be?" she wondered. "That's exactly what happened to my husband's grandfather!"

To make a long story short it turns out they were one and the same man, except my grandmother and my Aunt Estelle (whose name I carry) were progeny from his first marriage. After the death of their mother they went to live with relatives, a childless couple named Robinson that I vaguely remembered living in the Salt Springs area.

We managed to fill in a part of her son, Bill Tufts' genealogical research that day and my ties to St. Martins were made stronger.

All of which means nothing to anyone but me but it perhaps accounts in part for my interest in those famous ship builders and the men who sailed from St. Martins a century and more ago.

Phantom Ships and Sea Monsters

The Phantom of St. Martins

One of the most regularly chronicled "fire-ship" or "phantom ship" plies the Bay of Fundy, about two miles out from the Village of St. Martins, once a village of wealthy sea captains and ship builders.

The Bay of Fundy flows out from St. Martins for forty miles to the coast of Nova Scotia, the outline of which is most visible just before a storm. Frequently residents and visitors alike recount the sighting of a sailing vessel gliding across the bay, her rigging a mass of flames while figures, black against the blazing light, scurried around the deck.

It is believed to be the ghost of a ship that burned a hundred years ago, or more, off the coast. All on board were lost but every seven years since that time, usually in the fall of the year, it sails up the bay again.

Like the phantom ship of the Bay de Chaleur, St. Martins' burning vessel has made history for more than one hundred years and is still seen today. It is frequently described as being "a mass of flames" yet it never burns, and often sails up toward the head of the Bay of Fundy, in the vicinity of the Isle of Haute.

Isle Haute itself is steeped in stories of the sea, most particularly tales of Captain Kidd's pirate treasure said to be buried there. The island in itself, a small barren speck far out in the bay stands like a block of solid rock. According to stories told on the mainland the island shifts its position once in every seven years always, of course, on the stroke of midnight. That, of course, was the only lucky time to dig for the treasure. In truth, all the rules for digging pirate treasure must apply if one is to be successful. To date no one appears to have been. Perhaps they broke the silence when the blinding light flashed from the pit and the headless pirate sentry emerged and began to patrol his proscribed beat!

A favourite among Isle of Haute tales is that of the school master ... some say he was a farmer ... who decided to try his luck. There are those who tell the story today that claim he would have succeeded too, he was smart enough and brave enough, had it not been for his sweetheart who had learned where he had gone and followed him. She was, of course, concerned for his safety.

After following the rules of treasure digging the young man and his silent Indian helper persevered through rain, thunder and lightening that raged around them until at last their spades struck metal. From the depths a fiery guardian arose ... and a terrified shriek split the air.

The young woman swooned into her lover's arms, only to die there ... of fright presumably, and the terrified Indian rushed into the sea and was drowned. As for the young man he was found by a search party from the mainland, mindlessly wandering around the island. It is said he died soon afterward.

The late Ian Sclanders had a wonderful knack of turning a phrase and one time he wrote the following about Maritimers in general, New Brunswickers in particular and the effect the Bay of Fundy had on their imaginations.

"No shores have a larger share of bold tales than those of historic old Bay of Fundy. The earliest of course came from the Indians and naturally took on the mysterious and gigantic. Everything about the bay with its phenomenal rise and fall of tide, its bold, rocky bluffs, suggested to them the mighty and remarkable. The very fogs, magnifying objects, made them into walking men of great size. Each bush moved by the breeze was a strange figure and, in the ceaseless pounding of the tides, there was surely the voice of some great mysterious power."

Of course the newest residents of these shores, men and women from Europe or fleeing the rebellion in the United States to the south of us, soon developed legends of their own and Captain Kidd was responsible for a great many of those.

The stories of his selection of the shores of Fundy as a hiding place for his chests of gold was accepted and handed down through generations. Scores of excavations made by eager fortune seekers erupt at intervals as interest waxes and wanes, usually flaring up when someone, digging in a ditch somewhere, comes across a few old coins.

There are, of course, many fantastic tales of midnight appearances and hair-raising experiences in specific areas, among them Hopewell Hill in Albert County.

It was here that the infamous Captain Kidd is said to have beheaded a horseman, leaving him there to guard his treasure. Unsuccessful treasure-hunters reinforced the stories of the disembodied horseman, often claiming to have been thwarted by his dedication to duty!

People continue to look for buried treasure in some strange places. One Albert County man is said to have opened his store one morning only to find that someone during the previous night had unearthed a huge boulder embedded under the floor, in the belief that the boulder covered pirates' loot.

The Phantom Fire Ship
of the Bay of Chaleur

Fire ships and ghost ships have been watched in awe for centuries by men, women and children along every coast of New Brunswick. Of these the most famous is the Phantom Ship of Bay de Chaleur. Its sightings and its stories have been chronicled by historians and storytellers for more than a century, although there are some who dare to disclaim it as a mere mirage.

Of course no one takes any stock of these spoilers! As New Brunswickers we take great pride in our mysteries and our ghosts. We do not care to have them solved or explained. Most wags will agree there is an element of truth in the stories. Certainly it has been proven beyond doubt that there is some mystery as yet unsolved in the sightings of a light on the Bay de Chaleur and that that light could, quite easily, be taken for a burning, full-rigged ship.

Scientifically-minded people who have made a study of the phenomenon regard it as some type of natural occurrence which manifests itself in such a way as to be imagined as a vessel on fire. The romantics insist on spinning stories of pirates, historical personages and other fantasies.

There are those who claim that frequently at night, before a storm, a large light can be seen on the surface of the bay. This light knows no season for it has been seen in winter when ice covers the bay and in summer when the water is blue and tranquil.

Nor does this phenomenon restrict itself to any one part of the bay although at times it is reported brighter than at other times and it has often appeared to dance along the surface. There are those who say it is so bright that it could light up houses on the shore and even those who doubt the phantom ship's presence have been known to admit there were nights when the mysterious light gave off rays that shot into the gloom, appearing for all the world like the flame-lit rigging of a vessel.

Others have reported seeing the phantom of the bay in a number of places at once, on the ice off Clifton, for example, and about ten miles away behaving in a very peculiar manner, dying away one moment to a barely discernible speck of light then mounting up the next minute into a bright column of brilliance about thirty feet high.

One person reported seeing it while sailing on the bay one dark night. The light appeared ahead of the boat and, as they sailed towards it it became quite clear. They passed about a hundred yards to one side of the light and, from the decks, watchers could see that the light resembled a half-moon laying on the water with the flat side down and glowing like a hot coal.

Most commonly it has been reported in the form of a ship, often a whale boat, sometimes a column and sometimes appearing like an ordinary bonfire. Among those who have seen the phantom more than once it has been agreed that the shape of the phantom light would often change. Many also believed that its appearance heralded a storm, a belief that received confirmation from a Harvard University professor who was visiting the district nearly 100 years ago.

This professor said he saw the light one night and its appearance was followed by a violent northwester ... but it could have been a mere coincidence ... Who knows?

The professor's curiosity was aroused and, on making enquiries he found that similar lights had been reported in the Gulf of St. Lawrence and as far south as the Northumberland Straits. (We also happen to know it has occurred in St. Martins, but that's another story!)

The learned gentleman, however, came to the conclusion that, while most of the local stories had quite a few embellishments there was some basis for the tales. That, in truth, there does occur in that district some kind of light along the general nature of St. Elmo's light.

Similar phenomena have been claimed in other parts of the world, notably Wales, but none are as large nor as consistent performers as the one in New Brunswick's Bay de Chaleur.

Groups of reliable and sober citizens have been known to watch the phenomenon for up to two hours before it faded away, gradually, from the top down.

As early as 1875 fire storms were reported in the bay and in 1880 residents of the area attending a dance responded to the call of "fire storm!" and rushed out to view the spectacle only to be so terrified that the party broke up early and almost everyone went home!

Just what the phantom ship is a phantom of is a question with many answers. There are those who maintain it is the Lady Colbourne, a sailing schooner which at the time, 1838, was loaded to the gunnels with gold, silver, sperm oil and spices not to mention a large cargo of fine wines and spirits. The passengers, too, were persons of wealth presumed to have been either decked out in or in possession of valuable jewelry.

It is said that forty-three people drowned in the catastrophe and that when the body of one of the passengers washed up on shore a thousand pounds in bank notes were found on her body.

Then there are always the stories of pirate ships when

such phenomena occur, even sightings of a kidnapped Indian maiden said to have put a curse on the ship.

Too numerous to relate here are other stories of fact or fiction that continue to be spun over the years. One, that talks of the vessel being a British or French warship floats vaguely around in my memory, is itself a phantom. In this narrative some eyewitnesses are believed to have stayed hidden among some brush near the shore and watched as a longboat, carrying four soldiers and several mysterious boxes, was rowed ashore. Under the direction of an officer the soldiers dug a trench and buried the boxes before returning to the longboat and heading back to their ship.

The watchers either beat a hasty retreat or failed to find the buried boxes. I honestly don't remember which and have never read or heard this particular story again!

Ghost Ships ply rivers, too

In his book "*Ghosts Pirates and Treasure Trove, the Phantoms that haunt New Brunswick*" published in 1975 by McClelland and Stewart, Stuart Trueman writes of a mysterious Viking ship that sails across the mouth of the Shiktahauwk where it flows into the St. John river.

According to a legend told around camp fires on dark nights in the Bristol area, a party of treasure seekers had just struck a wooden object with their shovels when they were startled by strange sounds coming from across the river. The men watched wide-eyed and speechless as a Viking ship came sailing towards them "its elevated prow slicing swiftly through the waters and sending out waves on both sides."

Before retreating in terror they had glimpsed figurehead dragons rising terrifyingly from the bows and the stern while round shields armoured the long boat's sides and the bearded chieftain in "winged Norse helmet with long hair streaming behind" lead a raucous chorus of foreign battle songs.

At Jacquet River on the North Shore of the province people have been digging for treasure for nearly two centuries in an area traditionally called The Island.

According to local folklore two brothers both, of course, staunch God-fearing churchmen were checking out a site early in the nineteenth century when they were surprised by a boat that kept coming toward them without any sign of man or sail power. When it reached the sand bar it sailed across it as easily as it had across the water and beached itself beside the two men.

There were six men on board, obviously foreigners for they spoke neither French nor English, and they indicated by sign that they wanted food and shelter.

They then proceeded to stay at a Jacquet River boarding house and inn for several days in plain sight of villagers, yet no one ever saw when or how they left.

The Kennebecasis River has also had its share of ghost ships, one of which is explained by Trueman who tells how some treasure hunters were tricked by exuberant workers on the European and North American Railway who happened on them one dark night.

The men had been drinking at a tavern in Saint John and had missed the supply train ride back to where they were working in Rothesay. Rather than walk the ten miles they hired a boat and took the water route instead. As they came around a spit of land they could see the lanterns and three shadowy figures digging on shore. Silently they continued rowing their boat toward shore until suddenly they were seen by the treasure seekers who screamed in terror, certain the ghosts guarding the buried treasure were coming to get them.

The railway gang gathered up the lanterns and other paraphernalia and dumped it all in the hole and buried it. Later they were intrigued by the stories of how treasure hunters were on the verge of finding Captain Kidd's gold when suddenly a ghostly boat full of blood thirsty pirates came racing towards them, intent on killing to protect the treasure.

The Phantom Ship
of Kennebecasis Bay

Back in the 1940s, just after the Second World War, a radio program on CHSJ called the SMT Family Almanac was broadcast twice a week on Tuesdays and Saturdays. I don't know who did the research and wrote the scripts but whoever it was collected a true jewel box of treasures. Many of these treasures have been gathered by later writers and kept in circulation.

In one of the series I discovered a phantom ship that was certainly new to me, although it may be well known in one form or another to the people who have lived for years on Kennebecasis Bay. A Bay which, according to the narrator "rivals in its placid beauty and romantic surroundings many a world famous sheet of water (and) is the scene of some mysterious legends and tales.

"It is said that in one of its secluded coves, the masts of a sunken ship, abandoned by the French during their occupation of the country more than two hundred years ago, have often been seen still standing upright in its transparent depths.

"Along the western shore of the bay buried treasure has been sought and, it is said, not without success.

"Phantom boats have been reported at frequent intervals, scudding from point to point in the bright moonlight, under a full press of canvas, although the air was so still that not a ripple appeared on the glassy surface of the bay nor a leaf stirred in the trees that overhung its shores.

"A long dead but very reputable resident of one of the bay's sunshiny hamlets avers that at one time, when he was crossing from Henderson's Cove to Sandy Point in the early morning hours, he was pursued by a devil with glaring eyes and sulphur-breathing nostrils.

"There were witnesses whose honesty could not be questioned who affirmed that this nocturnal boatman was found in the bottom of his boat at Sandy Point in the early morning, wholly insensible through terror."

There are some who may question who or what the demons responsible for the above mentioned man's "insensible terror" were but who are we to question such authoritative folklore?

The story teller continued to weave his tale of the beauty of the St. John River, its waterscapes and landscapes until, reaching the area between Gagetown and Fredericton, he weaves this ghostly tale.

"Between Gagetown and Fredericton the islands in the St. John are numerous and varied in form and aspect. The islands, as seen ahead, as they come into being close at hand, and as they fade into the distance, are, with their beautiful scenery and even more beautiful surroundings, the perfect spots for such a legend as the Island of the Seven Cities ....

"It appears that many centuries ago, when the world was full of romance, belief was given to a legend that somewhere in the vicinity of the Canaries, there existed an island, the Island of the Seven Cities, where life was immortal and sorrows never came. This island was sought by many navigators, but though they sometimes caught glimpses of its shadowy shores it always receded on their near approach, and at last vanished completely, leaving the searchers to abandon their fruitless quest.

"Once it was reached, so the legend says, by one don

Fernando de Ulmo of Lisbon who, after spending a day and night, so he supposed, in the enjoyment of its many delights was picked up at sea by a passing vessel and taken to his home port of Lisbon. But it was not the Lisbon he knew. His friends had been in their graves for a hundred years or more and when he asked for the Senoritas he used to know, he was looked upon as a madman, and directed to the crumbling monuments that marked their graves.

While it is not likely that a similar fate will befall those who set foot upon the island pearls that dot the St. John River, the myths of the Island of Seven Cities might find an even better locale on some island of the St. John than on a bit of land in the middle of the Atlantic Ocean ....″

Ann Currier, Quaco's Ghost Ship

It was Dec. 5, 1883 when the Ann Currier cleared New York with a cargo of Christmas merchandise destined for Saint John. She sailed under Capt. William Vanwart and four crew including George Peck and Leonard Vanwart and two unnamed seamen. She was off the Nantucket Shoals when the crew of a fishing ketch noticed her lurching aimlessly and "acting might funny."

Wondering what was wrong the fishermen manoeuvred alongside and hailed her but there was no answer. In fact there was no sign of life at all. Although her foresail and jib were down and all was in good order when the fishermen boarded her, they could not find a soul on board. Nothing was missing save the captain, the crew and the lifeboat.

The fishermen took her into Vineyard Haven and the company that insured her paid them for salvage. H.R. Ranney of St. John, who represented the insurance company hired a crew in Boston to bring the Ann Currier from Vineyard Haven to St. John. A Capt. Beverly was in command.

The captain and his crew brought her into the Bay of Fundy and would have reached St. John if a heavy gale hadn't blown up from the southwest, sweeping her beyond her destination. The captain finally anchored in the shelter of Quaco Head.

The night of Jan. 18,1884 the wind hauled around to the southeast and, dragging anchor, the schooner piled up on White Rocks. At low tide she was high and dry.

Capt. Beverly and his crew got ashore but left with what some people saw as rather undue haste under the circumstances. They hired a team on Jan. 19 to take them to Saint John and they were shipped back to the United States immediately.

When the residents of Quaco went aboard the vessel they found the panelling of her cabin chopped away with an axe, boards and splinters lay all over.

What, if anything, was hidden behind that panelling? Where did the original crew that sailed from New York in December of 1883 go? More than a century has passed without word of Captain VanWart and his crew.

One can't help but wonder if there was something special in that Christmas shipment, something so special that it was worth abandoning ship and disappearing forever.

Did someone else board the ship on the coast of Massachusetts, unknown to Captain or crew, murder them and make a safe getaway without finding what Capt. Beverly and his crew discovered later?

One can easily imagine a number of variations on these themes!

The Union
Mystery Ship of St. Martins

In 1889 four unemployed St. Martins ship carpenters, John Kelly, George Cutten, Michael Kelly and Nathaniel MacCumber decided to build a ship on their own. They named her the Union.

On her maiden voyage, under the command of Capt. John Kelly, she delivered a cargo of piling to Boston then set sail through the Gulf of Maine to pick up lumber at Shulie, Nova Scotia. As she reached the Bay of Fundy Capt. Kelly put into the breakwater at St. Martins so the crew of four, Frank McDonough, William Bradshaw, Nelson Smith and Jack Dyre could have a chance to visit their families before making for Shulie.

Jack Dyre, who had no family in St. Martins, volunteered to stand watch while the others went ashore. On the Monday morning when they reported back to the ship McDonough, Bradshaw and Smith found Dyre standing on the breakwater, his luggage piled beside him. A terrified Dyre told the following story:

Around 10 o'clock on the Sunday night he turned into his bunk. All was peaceful and he quickly fell asleep. Some time later he was awakened from a deep sleep with a start. A voice was warning him to leave the ship.

Suspecting a prank he searched in vain for the source of the voice and finally decided that he must have been dreaming. He crawled back in his bunk and was soon fast

31

asleep once more, only to be rudely awakened a second time by the same voice giving a warning.

Again he toured *The Union* from stem to stern without locating a source for the voice.

When, for the third time, the same ominous voice roused him from sleep he was severely shaken. He quickly packed his meagre belongings and scurried off the ship to await the return of the captain and the crew on the breakwater.

Despite Capt. Kelly's entreaties he refused to step foot on the deck of the Union ever again. Kelly was forced to pay him off and signed on William Bradshaw's relative, Richard Bradshaw, to complete the Union's voyage to Shulie.

Dropping away from the breakwater with the tide at noon *The Union* drifted toward Shulie. As the tide ebbed the Union was once more abeam of St. Martins, surrounded by forty other becalmed vessels.

Black clouds gradually accumulated but there was still no wind by the end of the afternoon. Keeping an eye on the weather Capt. Kelly walked into the galley, remarked that it looked like rain and prepared to don his oilskins.

Suddenly *The Union* gave a violent roll and, a moment later, seemed to be falling through space. Capt. Kelly could hear the voice of McDonough below, telling everyone to come up on deck. The Union had capsized, turning completely over.

Smith, who had been with Capt. Kelly in the galley had dashed up the companionway as the ship went over and was able to leap free. Capt. Kelly, trapped in the galley, drew a deep breath and dived into the companionway which by now was pointing down, rather than up! He surfaced at the side of the ship and Smith, who was clinging to the keel, reached out and helped the captain to safety.

A black cloud hovering directly overhead pelted them with heavy rain as they clung desperately to the keel, searching in vain for their companions.

The Union had gone over so fast she was still full of compressed air and Kelly and Smith were treated to a fuselage of reports like pistol shots as the oakum blew out of her seams.

Fishermen rowed out in a small boat when the rain stopped, rescuing Kelly and Smith. Eventually she was towed ashore where she was righted and repaired to sail on for nearly twenty eight years before being wrecked in a storm at the mouth of the Bay of Fundy in 1917. A French gunboat eventually sunk the abandoned vessel which posed a menace to navigation.

Apparently of the more than forty vessels becalmed that night the Union was the only one to have "turned turtle." Historian Frederick Cochrane interviewed the survivors who told him no one ever solved the mystery of why she overturned. It was one of those strange events that everyone claims just couldn't have happened, but it did.

Nor has anyone ever solved the phenomenon of the eerie voice that forced Jack Dyre off the ship and, obviously, saved his life.

Just one more unsolved mystery of the sea.

Eat your heart out, Nessie

Any New Brunswicker labouring under the impression that Scotland has the corner on sea monsters just doesn't know their province's history.

The earliest report I have come across occurred in 1838 and other reports continue to the present day. There are times when I wonder if the sea monster of 1838 and another monster, that literally continues to surface on a regular basis, aren't either one and the same sea monster or descendants thereof ... albeit that they appear to exist in different locations.

Our 1838 monster has only been sighted the once, to my knowledge, in the Bay of Fundy but if the description of the creature is accurate then once is enough!

The credibility of the creature's reported size might be questioned were it in any other inland water but, considering the 40 ft. high tides and the tremendous depth of the Bay of Fundy, the door is definitely open to speculation that the stories are true.

Personally, I don't doubt for a minute the possibility of its existence.

The largest of most sea monsters tend to run in the vicinity of 50 ft. or so, or nearly twice the length of the average modern bungalow. That's pretty big to meet face to face as it were, particularly when you're sitting in a dory!

Sea monsters are described as being typically serpent-like in that they resemble dinosaurs but sport scaly snake-like skin and have paddle feet.

On a calm and pleasant day in the summer of 1883 residents of a small French community named Mantagon, near Yarmouth, NS, were thrown into a state of shock when several fishermen of the village reported sighting what could only be described as a sea serpent in the Bay of Fundy.

A second group of people, enjoying a pleasure boating day on the water not only sighted this phenomenon but had a terrifying close-up view of it.

At first they spotted what they presumed to be a large fish, perhaps a shark or a whale, gliding through the water toward them. It was producing a wake in the water similar to that which a boat under sail would make.

As this supposed fish approached they discovered that the creature gliding toward their boat was neither a large fish nor a whale. It was a huge sea monster that appeared to stretch from one hundred to one hundred and fifty feet in length. The creature's head, held somewhat erect as it glided steadily toward them, was the circumference of a large barrel.

They stood frozen in terror, watching something that defied any other description save that of a sea serpent or sea monster pass majestically within an oar's length of the boat ... ignoring them completely as it silently headed up the bay on the tide.

When they returned to shore to share their excitement they discovered that numerous fishing crews had returned home early, having experienced the same sighting and corroborating the group's evidence.

Now the only other such creature anywhere near the Bay of Fundy that I am aware of is the monster said to inhabit Lake Utopia, a large lake located between Saint

John and St. George.

I can remember, as a child, going to visit friends of my parents who had a cottage far down the lake from the dirt road leading into the shore of the lake at that time. In order to reach their cottage we were required to traverse the length of the lake in a row boat. Having heard stories of the monster we travelled the distance in some trepidation, keeping our eyes open for suspicious ripples and wakes.

Each time we made this trip I faced the adventure with both fear and excitement. Never mind that my parents constantly assured me that it was "just a story." I knew better. I had asked the man who owned the row boat that ferried us down the lake if the sea monster really did exist and he assured me that it did, indeed, but went on to tell me not to worry. He claimed he had seen the monster itself and, being local, could always tell when it was going to surface.

He even told me what to watch for.

"If you're in the water playing and the water suddenly seems to be a lot deeper that it was when you first went in, that's a sign! Get back on the beach, fast!"

Sage advice, I realize now. Monster or no monster!

Every time I went in the water I watched for signs of the sea serpent. Sometimes when the water suddenly got deeper I would scurry back to shore, waiting and watching but nothing happened.

To this day I am sure that sea monster was lurking there somewhere in the depths of the lake, perhaps in an underwater cavern. I don't profess to know the life-span of giant sea serpents but I wonder if it was either the same one that was in the Bay of Fundy or was it, perhaps, a descendant. Think about it. Lake Utopia is not that far from the Bay of Fundy coast and anyone around there will tell you that the area is pocketed with caves and underground rivers.

Perhaps the reason that sea serpent monster hasn't been seen since 1838 in the Bay of Fundy is because it sailed into one of those caves, followed an underground river into Lake Utopia where it and/or its descendants have been hanging out ever since.

Eat your heart out, Nessie. New Brunswick may be nurturing a couple of generations of sea monsters somewhere in the bowels of the earth where unknown rivers flow!

Horror Stories and Hauntings at Sea

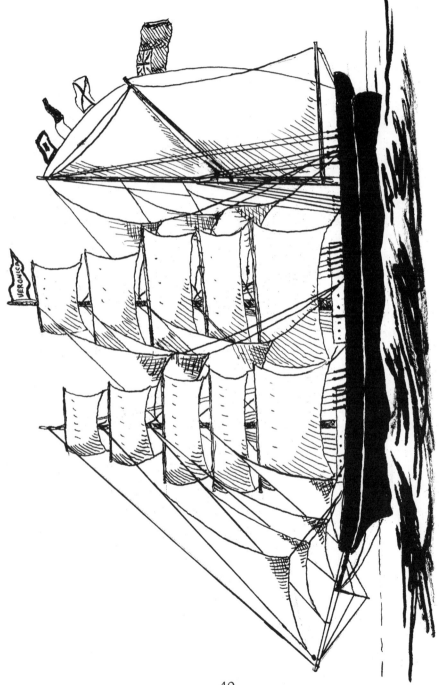

Power struggle on the fo'c'sle creates horror on the high sea

The barque *Veronica* was built at the Rowan shipyard in Saint John in 1879. She was 186.4 feet long with a beam of 37.8 feet and a 22.1 feet hold. Saint John was her home port and she was owned by Thompson and Company.

She was still a sturdy and reliable vessel in October of 1902 when she left Biloxi, Mississippi carrying a cargo of hard pine lumber destined for Montevideo, Uruguay, South America. Captain Alexander Shaw, a veteran of a lifetime at sea was at the helm although by this time he was somewhat impaired by extreme deafness.

Captain Shaw was considered a stern, cruel master by many sailors who had shipped with him yet, at home in Saint John, he was known as a kindly old man.

The trouble on the *Veronica* began when two crew members, Pat Doran and Gustav Rau, wanted the prestige and benefits that came from the privilege of running the forecastle gang. The battle was an ugly affair but Doran got the nod and assumed the honours of the position.

Rau carried a deep and determined grudge, fed regularly by two fellow Germans on board, Otto Monsson and Harry Flohr who believed their race was affronted by the appointment. They convinced a Dutch crewman, Willem Smith to side with them and the four spent many hours chewing on their grievance until, ultimately, they concluded the only solution to the situation was to kill Doran.

Rau was becoming more and more paranoid and he convinced himself and the others that Doran was actually in league with Captain Shaw, Chief Mate Alexander McLeod of Prince Edward Island and Second Mate Fred Abrahamson of Sweden in a plot to make life on board so bad for the four that they would jump ship at the next port.

The quality of the food on board was seen as a deliberate attempt to debilitate them.

The Veronica was becalmed on the outer fringe of the Doldrums, near Brazil, on the night of Sunday, December 2. Doran was standing on the fo'c'sle head when suddenly Rau pulled out his knife and handed it to Flohr with instructions to "Stick it in Paddy's throat!"

The young Flohr started to cry in protest so Rau and Smith decided to rid themselves of Doran on their own. With Flohr trailing behind them they climbed to the f'oc's'le armed with belaying pins hidden behind their backs.

Rau surprised Doran by making friendly chatter which put him completely off guard. When Doiron crouched to peer under the foot of the foresail to check the position of the North Star Rau and Smith smashed him on the head with the belaying pins.

Doran tried to protect himself but he was soon knocked unconscious and stuffed into the port paint-locker.

Chief Mate McLeod heard the scuffle and rushed forward to see what was happening.

"Who's on lookout?" he asked Rau.

Rau told him Doran had been there but they saw him fighting with someone.

McLeod hurried forward to check out the situation only to be struck a series of violent blows from the two Germans when he approached.

Rau found a revolver in McLeod's pocket and promptly pocketed it for himself before ordering McLeod to be thrown overboard.

Rau and his buddies decided the time had come to take over the entire vessel.

The captain, shot in the stomach and injured from the belaying pin attack, managed to lock himself in the chart-room where he was soon joined by the Second Mate, also shot in the stomach by Rau.

Rau and the others then nailed wood over the port-holes, roped down the skylight and fastened timbers across the door of the chart room entrance, making the Captain and Second Mate prisoners.

Doran was still alive and complaining of thirst so they threw him overboard then went looking for the cook, Thomas. Rau was all set to murder him but Smith said he was needed to prepare the meals, Rau gave in and set Thomas to boiling coffee for them.

By December 11 Rau decided it was time to deal with the men in the chart room. There hadn't been any more killings and presumably life had become dull for him. The Captain offered him his gold watch in return for some water then Rau nailed the hatch down again while he decided what to do with the men.

Three days later he ordered them up on deck. The mate made it up and was promptly shot in the shoulder by Smith. In desperation and resignation the mate jumped over the side and was never seen again.

Rau got tired of waiting for the Captain to come on deck and sent a man down to "chase him up" with an axe. Once the Captain was on deck Rau ordered young Flohr to shoot him but Flohr wouldn't, or couldn't, finally Rau took the gun from him and did the job himself: blowing the captain's brains out as he leaned against the hatchway, his hands before his face.

After declaring himself "Captain" of the *Veronica,* Rau named Smith his lieutenant and designated Monsson, Thomas, Flohr, and Bravo as the crew.

Originally the mutineers had intended to wreck the *Veronica* then they decided to burn her … but not before Rau had created a scenario in which the crew was diligently rehearsed. "Captain" Rau knew it was important for them to tell a believable tale, one that would explain the missing captain, mates and crew members.

With the skill a Hollywood script writer might envy, backed by regular rehearsals under his direction, Rau turned his crew into consummate actors. They all knew if they failed in their command performance the alternative was sure death.

They were instructed to tell a tale of how the Veronica had experienced bad weather after reaching the Florida Straits resulting in the main top-sail-yard being carried away. Chief Mate McLeod, in attempting to repair it, had fallen to the deck and been killed.

The next disaster to attack the crew was the onslaught of dreaded yellow fever which claimed the lives of the Second Mate and two of the crew. The next tragedy hit shortly after the men had been sent to their watery grave … the Veronica was becalmed off the Brazilian coast when, for some unknown reason, fire broke out amidships and everyone, including the Captain, was forced to abandon the barque. Part of the crew, including Rau and the present crew, got into the longboat while the Master and the others took the quarter-boat.

Unfortunately two of the crew, Bravo and Johanssen, were intellectually challenged and could not memorize their lines correctly. Rau despaired of ever getting his show on the road. Fearing that the two would cause his production to fail on its first performance he decided they would have to die.

It was script-writing time again.

Rau ordered Johanssen out to stow the flying-jib which was hanging below the boom. Johanssen crawled out on the boom then, when he was on the bowsprit, Rau and Smith used him for target practice. Riddled with bullets Johanssen fell overboard.

Next Rau ordered Bravo to haul up the slack of the foresheet which was trailing in the water. As Bravo hauled in the sail Smith went behind him and shot him in head and Bravo fell into his watery grave.

Flohr, the sixteen year old who had failed in his part as terminator earlier in the script now became stage-struck and vied for a bigger part in the production. He decided to take out Thomas, the cook and aimed his pistol at the man's head but before he could shoot Smith stayed his hand.

"Who's going to cook for us if you kill him?"

This was twice the cook's life was spared. Ironically Rau's production might have played had Thomas been killed.

Julius Parsons, one of the original crew who refused to take part in the activities had been locked in the deckhouse. That midnight he decided to try and escape. He got his head and shoulders through the small, square window but became stuck and was found there by Monsson who cheerfully battered the man to death with his belaying pin.

By now Rau was sure he had a success on his hands. He set Moses Thomas, the cook, to work baking bread and provisioning the longboat for a long journey, in addition to chopping plenty of kindling wood. This was then piled on the deck and covered with mattresses, old clothing and kerosene.

Once the longboat was fully provisioned they lowered it over the side before lighting the pyre. The four crew and the cook then shoved off in the long boat. Before setting sail for the coast of Brazil they dallied nearby, watching fascinated as the *Veronica* went up in flames.

On Christmas Day they threw provisions, hats and incriminating evidence overboard then threw themselves on the mercy of the Captain of the steamer *Brunswick*, out of

Liverpool.

Rescued, they set sail for England having given what they believed to be a stellar performance for the *Brunswick's* Captain and crew. But Rau made a bad mistake en route. One dark night he attempted to reach Thomas, who was bunked with the *Brunswick's* cook, presumably to either threaten or kill him.

Whatever Rau's intent, he succeeded in scaring Thomas enough that the cook decided the time had come for him to put on his own one-man show.

From the beginning the *Brunswick's* captain was suspicious of the tale he had been told by Rau and his troupe. When Thomas came to him with his story of mutiny and murder he believed him. While they were on the high sea however, there was little the Captain could do about the situation. The *Brunswick's* staterooms were filled with passengers, among them numerous women and children and the Captain feared what Rau might do among his own crew. He decided to treat the mutineers with courtesy and generosity until he could reach a safe harbour and turn them over to the authorities.

His ruse succeeded. The mutinous four had no suspicions at all until, after docking in Liverpool, the police boarded the *Brunswick* to interview them.

Moses Thomas told his story again to the authorities and Flohr, frightened of what might happen to him, decided to come clean. He did not know at the time that Thomas had already told his story twice, now Flohr's story was all the confirmation the police needed.

Rau and Smith, in a last-ditch attempt to save the show, tried to put the blame on Flohr and Thomas but they were doomed to fail. Rau and Smith and Monsson were charged and found guilty of the killing of Alexander Shaw, master of the *Veronica*, and of piracy on the high seas.

On May 15, 1903 the jury took twelve minutes to find

them guilty. Rau and Smith were hanged but 18 year-old Monsson, who had a clean record until then, was recommended to mercy. Flohr, having given King's evidence went free.

Captain Browne of the *Brunswick* was complimented on his behaviour and received 10 guineas as a reward.

New Brunswick Sea Stories

Cannibalism on the Caroline

For those who love to shiver at a story ... and maybe give themselves nightmares ... the story *Cannibalism on the Caroline*, as told by A.J. McCarthy in his book *Bay of Chaleur Forgotten Treasures,* is virtually guaranteed to do that.

The *Caroline*, a barque out of Joseph Cunard's shipyard in Bathurst in 1839, was caught and wrecked in a gale off Savannah, Georgia in 1847. Some of the crew were washed overboard. Those who remained were both hungry and thirsty, having gone without food for fifteen days and without water for eight days. Not for the first time in the history of disaster the survivors decided that, if they were to survive, cannibalism was their only resort .

The Captain offered himself for slaughter but the crew drew lots and ... Surprise! Surprise!... the most chubby man of the lot was the loser. He was not a willing victim and defended himself with a knife.

According to McCarthy's tale the Captain spotted an adze partly under water and had a young Welsh boy bring it to him. He then went on deck with the boy, what his intentions were it is difficult to fathom but what happened was that the chubby dinner designate attacked the boy, with the idea that the lad would be his stand-in. Before he could stab him the Captain attacked with the adze and the crew sustained themselves on the body for three days.

On November thirteenth the survivors, all three of them:

the Captain, the Mate and the Welsh boy, were discovered by a brig bound for Connecticut.

One can't help but wonder how many there were when the cannibalism began.

... or how many would have been left if the *Tampice* hadn't picked them up when it did!

Blood, gore and more tales of old ship's at sea

New Brunswick's North Shore appears either to be blessed or, some would say, cursed with stories of blood, gore and ghosts on both sea and shore. The story of the Squando, a Norwegian barque that was tied up at the Bathurst wharf around the turn of the century has been chronicled almost as often as the phantom fire ship of Chaleur Bay.

No fewer than three writers of sea stories have offered up versions of the whys and wherefores of the vessel's hauntings. All have told the same classic tale with variations on the theme. The latest of these may be found in A. J. McCarthy's book *Bay of Chaleur Forgotten Treasures.*

According to McCarthy's research the trouble all began in Oslo, Norway when the captain brought a woman on board, a harbinger of bad luck.

The first night on board was an auspicious occasion to be sure. The crew were gathered in the main cabin when suddenly a hand spike flew through the air and struck the bulkhead. They left quickly, already complaining of jinxes and bad luck.

Later another spike embedded itself in the deck timbers, after that the men locked themselves in their cabins and kept every lantern on the ship burning through the night. Nevertheless when the intrepid dared peer out to the decks their frightened eyes beheld a headless man pacing the decks.

Hiding under the bedclothes was a useless precaution since the bedclothes were whipped from the beds during the night while a cold hand was said to touch their faces and an eerie voice encouraged them to leave ship and never return.

Many did just that.

The crew was relieved when they finally dropped anchor in San Francisco but it was a short lived relief because the schooner was no sooner tied to her moorings when the fracas began.

Apparently a bitter argument between the captain, his wife and the mate and, according to one story, the captain ultimately attacked the mate and lashed him to the mast.

Here the story varies from teller to teller. There are those who say the mate was beaten with an iron bar by the woman while the captain stabbed him repeatedly with a knife while the captain's wife joined the bloodlust crying, "I know how to stop the trouble on this ship!" and proceeded to attack the helpless mate with an axe, subsequently beheading him.

The mate was a big and strong man but he was overpowered and blood sprayed from vital arteries to soak ceiling, walls and floor as the vicious attack continued until the captain and his wife, exhausted and blood soaked stood back and viewed their handiwork in triumph.

They set about attempting to hide the evidence before the crew found them out but the crew had been expecting some kind of drama throughout the voyage and on hearing the fracas in the captain's cabin they sent for the police.

No recorded evidence to explain why the mate had been violently struck down has ever been discovered but there were rumblings among the crew to the effect that the captain's wife had made overtures to the mate and been rejected. No doubt he discovered too late that …

"Heaven has no rage like love to hatred turned
Nor Hell a fury like a woman scorned!"

From then on the ship was said not only to be haunted

but jinxed as well!

The new captain appointed to take over the Squando was promptly killed in a mutiny and the crew scattered as soon as they made port.

She was brought to Bathurst and another master was appointed but, after two weeks at sea, he died. From then on no officer or sailor would board the vessel and she was left tied up at Bathurst wharf.

On December 10, 1887 the *Chatham Gazette* reported:

"No more will Bathurst be agitated by the headless man of the haunted *Squando.* She met her fate during the heavy storms, and after lying stranded in the mud for almost a year she has been dashed ashore by the fury of gales, and is now all broken up. Captain Leel, who purchased the hull this last summer for forty dollars, is now at work saving the wreckage and it is expected he will clear a nice little sum by his speculation. The men engaged in the work were somewhat surprised to find, in between the timbers of the vessel, a bucket and an old metal axe."

New Brunswick Sea Stories

Murder at Sea

In her book *The Tides of Discipline,* writer and historian Ethel Thompson quoted a 1957 story told by Herbert Mawhinney of Chance Harbour.

Mawhinney was an able seaman on the three-masted American schooner *Alvarte S. Snare* which left Saint John at four o'clock on a Saturday afternoon November 12, 1899.

Another American schooner, the *J. B. VanDusen* left Saint John a half-hour later and the two vessels sailed past Musquash within sight of each other, taking advantage of a moderate nor'-east breeze. But the seeming serenity was deceiving. All was not well on board the *J.B. VanDusen.*

The Captain and a crew member got into an argument which developed into a physical struggle in the course of which the Captain was stabbed and fell overboard. The ship hove-to and a boat with two seamen was lowered, the body was recovered and taken into Dipper Harbour.

The *VanDusen* with a crew of two, the man who had stabbed the Captain and the cook, continued on its course along the coast. It was not long before the weather began to snow and blow and the men were forced to bring the ship to anchor in Beaver Harbour where they lay at anchor until the police arrived and arrested the seaman.

He was taken to Portland, Maine where he was tried for the murder of the captain and sentenced to eight years imprisonment. He told the court that he had been beaten up by the captain and taken aboard the vessel while drunk. When he got out to sea he sobered up and so the fight developed.

The *Alvarte* continued on and ran into a heavy snowstorm driven by a nor'east gale. After shortening sail the captain set course for Petite Manan on the Maine coast. He had set the course so accurately that they collided with the whistling buoy off Petite Manan Point.

Mawhinney was steering at the time and heard "a sort of rumble" and thought they had run ashore. Uncertainty did not last long, the vessel was rolling over the buoy and, when the buoy came up from under the stern, it let out such a roar that he "almost froze at the wheel." The ship began to leak and the sails began to blow away until only the jib and jumbo were left. The vessel was filled with water by then and there was nothing left but to run before the wind, a wind that headed them for Boston Bay and the dreaded Cape Cod shoals!

Before they reached the shoals the wind changed to nor'west and drove them off into the ocean instead. When they were about sixty-five miles southeast of Cape Cod the *Alvarte S. Snare* ceased to run before the gale and, instead, broached broadside to the sea and started to roll over.

The crew cut the masts and rigging in an attempt to keep the ship from upsetting. The masts went overboard followed by the deck load of six hundred pilings that broke loose. Just before they cut the masts the ship's anchors were washed overboard. They ran the full sixty-five fathoms of the anchor chains.

The ship came back when the deck load went overboard and, being full of water, the anchors acted as a drag which brought it head to the wind. Two-thirds of her forward part was submerged as the weight of the anchors held her there while the five hundred spruce pilings still in the hold kept her from sinking.

The only food was some canned peas and corn and a jug of water which were stored in the Captain's cabin. All the other food and water had been washed overboard with the cook's galley.

All day Monday they kept a sharp lookout, the only way to send distress signals was a flag during the day and a fire at night.

They had saved the ship's life boat and hoped to get off in it when the wind died down. The only shelter out of the water was the aft companionway of the Captain's cabin in which six were able to jam together and survive.

By midnight Monday they sighted the green and red lights of a schooner coming toward the wreck. They had taken a quilt out of the captain's cabin before dark and kept it, along with some matches, dry in the binnacle. Working fast they lashed the quilt to a pole with wire, soaked it in kerosene and set it on fire. When they lashed the pole to the davit "it lit up the ocean for quite a distance around and blinded us so we could not see the schooner lights!

"The fishing crew from Provincetown, Cape Cod on the *Joseph P. Johnston* had no trouble seeing us!"

They came close enough to hail them and told the crew to get into the lifeboat and they would send two dories to pick us up.

Despite two of the crew being disabled from exposure they got into the lifeboat and Mawhinney held the line to the wreck until the dories arrived to take the line.

"They banked us tandem to their vessel where we were taken aboard. Then, true to the tradition of the sea, they turned back from their fishing trip to George's Bank and brought us to Provincetown."

After the crew were fitted out with new clothes and their way paid to Boston by the Seaman's Aid Society the Captain and all but two of the crew, who were sent to hospital, were paid off by the ship's agents in Boston.

"We paid our own way back to Saint John," Mawhinney noted.

Iron Men and Wooden Ships

The Climb of a Lifetime

Although ships bigger than several football fields and fitted out with sensitive equipment make sailing up the Bay of Fundy to Saint John a ho-hum experience today it wasn't always so. It fact even today it isn't always such a pacific sail for fishermen, despite radar, sonar and, in some instances, the virtual reality of computerized charts.

Two particular areas, Grand Manan Island and Chance Harbour historically have contributed to the demise of many a vessel, some of them carrying merchandise of great value in its day and all carrying a full complement of fragile human beings.

The *Lord Ashburton*, built at Brandy Cove, St. Andrews by Briggs in 1843 was one of the many claimed by the rocks of Grand Manan.

She was a 1009 ton vessel over 155 feet long and about 30 feet in breadth with a depth of more than 22 feet. On Christmas Day, 1856 she entered the Bay of Fundy on her way to Saint John, having just completed an uneventful crossing of the Atlantic Ocean. Captain Owen Crerar of Pictou, N.S. sighted Grand Manan Island and expected to make port in a few days until he suddenly experienced his ship being buffeted first by strong head winds then a full force gale.

The *Lord Ashburton* was driven off her course and Captain Crerar was forced to retreat out to sea for safety. Time after time he tried to reach Saint John but the wind constantly forced him back out to sea again and each time, as if warning him of what was to come, the high cliffs of Grand Manan loomed up out of the storm always ominous, always threatening.

The temperature kept dropping and ice began to build up on the vessel and its rigging, waves sent icy spray higher than her highest mast, spray that froze on contact as it washed down the masts and decks.

It was with great relief that Captain Crerar finally sighted Partridge Island Light at the entrance to Saint John Harbour, and prayed that his problems were over. But it was not to be. The wind changed again and came in from the northeast and heavy snow blotted out all landmarks, including the light on Partridge Island. The waves began to build higher and higher, becoming stronger and stronger as they vented their winter fury on the ship.

By midnight the entire ship's company knew that a great northeast snowstorm had begun its siege. Only a few hours earlier they were nearly in safe harbour and looking forward to time with their families, now they feared for their lives.

By dawn the next day they couldn't see beyond the crashing waves and thick snow and the howling of the wind muffled their voices, shrieking at them like banshees of the ocean floor. They couldn't see where they were but they knew only too well. They knew the relentless wind was steadily pushing them toward destruction against the cliffs of Grand Manan.

The second day passed then, just after midnight the lookout heard the distant sound of breakers. He warned the captain of what lay ahead but there was nothing anyone could do but wait.

The booming and crashing of the surf against the rocks grew louder and louder, louder even than the crashing waves of the sea as it battered the *Ashburton*; louder even than the wind that whistled around the furled sails in the naked masts until, shuddering from stem to stern in a suicidal plunge it crashed against the rocks, .

Officers and crew huddled together on the starboard quarter knowing the uselessness of launching a lifeboat, waiting and praying, their fate unknown.

In its voracious hunger the sea sent huge hands to grasp a victim to its bottomless belly until only ten men remained of the original ship's company of twenty-nine.

One by one the survivors took their chances on the lee side of the storm, slipping into a wave, riding a piece of debris or swimming hoping to be carried to shore. Of the nine men who battled the waves the story of James Lawson is one of high drama, courage and a strong will to live.

Lawson, who was from Bornholm, Denmark, could hear his shipmates shouting but, like them, he was helpless in the waves which, in turn, engulfed him and drew him back to the sea then carried him triumphantly toward the rocks, tossing him toward shore. Back and forth he battled the sea as he sought, at each landfall, to gain a purchase that would hold him to the rocks.

Then a grandfather of all waves plucked him from his perch, picked him up and threw him up the cliff face. He shrieked in terror and, to his surprise, his cry was heard by a shipmate who by clamouring along the face of the cliff was able to grasp Lawson's hand and help him reach a shelf above the high tide mark.

Lawson rested there, exhausted, until the sun came up. The shipmate who had rescued him was nowhere to be seen!

Lawson looked up to the top of the cliff 300 feet above him. It was a climb he knew he would have to make before nightfall or he would freeze to death.

Fortunately the wind that the day before had tormented and tortured him now helped Lawson in his climb. The sixty and seventy miles an hour gale winds flattened him against the cliff face, enabling him to grasp and gain support from the most tiny of crevices until finally he reached the top.

Ahead of him were mound after mound of deep snow-drifts but he could see a building in the distance and, placing one blood foot ahead of the other, he made his way through the snow to the building where he collapsed in a mound of hay.

An hour or so later James Tatton, who lived nearby, decided to walk to the cliff and see what damage the storm had done. He discovered Lawson's bloody footprints and followed them to the barn.

The community rallied round and discovered six more survivors clustered at the foot of the towering cliff. After rescuing the six, the villagers returned to the cliff and mounted a search for other survivors. To their surprise they came around a ledge and saw a row of men sitting in a line along the beach and rushed to their aid.

There were twenty-two men in the row, facing out to sea, and every one of them was dead.

Lawson had all his toes and parts of his feet amputated and spent years in hospital before returning to Grand Manan where he took up the trade of .... would you believe it? ... shoemaker!

The stubborn Dane has become a legend on the island that became his home until his death on Feb. 22, 1918.

In the course of his lifetime there he was to meet yet another survivor of a wreck at the same location. In 1872 the *Sarah Sloane* was cast against the cliff with only one survivor, a Baltimore man named Charles Turner. Lawson befriended him and offered assistance when Turner, too, had his feet amputated.

New Brunswick Sea Stories

Tidal wave

One of the most frightening stories of the sea occurred in August of 1857 when what was considered then ... and would certainly still be considered now "a strange phenomenon called a tsunami or tidal wave" occurred in the Northumberland Strait and to some extent in the Bay de Chaleur.

It is believed that an underwater earthquake (a volcanic eruption was also considered) caused the sea to run to a height of fifty feet. One of the strangest aspects of the occurrence described by survivors was that the tops of those waves formed either a cone or "sugar loaf" shape.

In all about more than one hundred boats and thirty-five fishermen were lost, mainly off Shippagan and to some extent up the coast towards Bathurst. Of those boats that were on the top of the waves, one boat was said to have been hurled down like a boulder into the canyon formed by the swell.

Survivors spoke of being in thirty-five and forty fathoms of water with sand and gravel all around them being dredged up from the bottom. There were those who, tossed in the troughs maintained that their vessels "smelt bottom."

Wanted: One Rescue Team ... with Heart

Although the days of wooden ships were numbered with the advent of steam many continued to sail around the world and ply their trade amid the growing competition. One of the these, a 1,650 ton Russian barque named the Sovinto, was still industriously working in 1906 when it stopped in at Bathurst and Dalhousie to take on a load of deals. Laden with lumber and a large crew of twenty-one men, six of whom were from the Miramichi, it entered the Gulf of St. Lawrence and faced a huge storm blowing in from the northeast.

The storm was so strong that soon three of the Sovinto's masts were broken and lost overboard and she was driven ashore on a reef just off Prince Edward Island.

What followed was a disaster in which those iron men showed the stuff that made them famous and showed up the frailty of lesser individuals too chicken to do the duty for which they had been hired.

As the vessel was driven against the reef by gale force winds the men were forced from their cabins to the decks where the ship was pounded until it broke in two leaving three men on the forward part and seventeen on the after end where they clung for their lives throughout the night. One man, a Swede named Arthur Gjervic, jumped overboard as the ship struck the reef and was blown ashore as he clung, exhausted and near death to a floating plank where he managed to crawl up the beach.

The twenty remaining crew members clung either to the wreck or to a lifeboat launched by those on the afterdeck, suffering the buffeting of the waves and being dashed sometimes against the ship, sometimes the rocks. While they suffered from hunger, thirst, injury and exhaustion the governments of the day tossed, back and forth between them, the responsibility of a decision to send a rescue ship to their aid.

In the meantime the men were trying to save themselves and seven managed to make it ashore. One of the men, John Olsen, made it ashore while carrying an exhausted steward on his back. Unfortunately when they reached the surf the steward let go and was dashed against a rock and killed.

One private citizen became so enraged he dispatched a lifeboat by train to aid the struggling seamen but eventually one of three government cruisers in Charlottetown harbour, the *Stanley*, was sent to the rescue. After getting about halfway to the dying men the captain turned back, claiming the sea was too rough.

Finally a group of Prince Edward Island volunteers, risking their own lives, climbed aboard a double dory and rowed to the rescue of the men. They were able to rescue two of the men on the forward part. One of the three men left in the aft finally jumped in the water and managed to get ashore with the help of a floating deal. Others who tried the same thing were not so fortunate.

The three government ships; Minto, Stanley and Brant remained safe and sound in port all this time. A guilty government sent each survivor a sympathy note and thirty dollars.

New Brunswick Sea Stories

One of those Iron Men

Imagining life in the days of the wooden ships made by New Brunswick's earliest entrepreneurs is just one aspect of our turbulent relationship with the sea. Not only did our fame as superb shipbuilders spread around the world, our fame as sailors of brilliance whose strength and durability in the ongoing battle with the sea more than matched that of our ships.

One of these men was George McAllister, the seventh son of John McAllister, a lumberman and shipowner from Milltown on the U.S. – Canada border in Charlotte County. He was born in 1804 and, on February 16, 1842 at the age of 38, he was washed overboard in a storm and gale off the shore of Nova Scotia.

George McAllister's life and death were probably fairly typical of what we know of his era. Fortunately, he was not only a good sailor but a literate man of some depth. The following is copied from a part of *The Journal of Captain George C. McAllister, January 1, 1831 to July 27, 1833*. Published in 1958 from his original notes copied by Mary Hill in January of 1931, with introduction and further notes by Evans Hill.

I recommend it for fascinating reading. The copy I used is from the Saint John Regional Library, one of probably a very few still extant.

In just this brief passage one is able to visualize what life must have been like at sea day-after-day, year-after-year. Canvas sail, brute strength and inner stamina were the engines driving our wooden ships thousands of kilometres through gales and storms, fair weather and foul.

Memorandum of Events of 1831
by George C. McAllister

<u>*Jan. 1831*</u>

*Note 1s*t The brig *Keziah* under my charge lying at Upton's Wharf loading.

Very mild weather for the season, wind South Eastwardly.

Note 2nd Sunday. Attended Divine Service at the Methodist Chapel. Rev. Williams, Minister. Louisa married at 6 p.m. by Dr. Thompson.

The brig in the care of Wm. Harper, Mate. W. northwestwardly.

3rd. This day finished taking on the Deck load of Shingles, it being seven bunches in height, loading done, dropped down to the Ledge to prevent being froze in, anchored at the Ledge at 6 p.m. and returned home with Father in the carriage.

Note 4th. Remained at home all this day it being cold, and much ice running in the River. Sent Horatio N. Hill to the Ledge to assist in looking after the Brig, while the Mate went to St. Andrews for his clothes.

5th. Rode down to the Ledge to see about getting some small jobs done to the vessel necessary before going to sea. Wind Southwardly.

6th. Rode down upon the American side and crossed over to Saint Andrews in the Brig's boat, to clear out for sea and ship two men, which done, crossed over to Robinstown in the evening and returned home, leaving the boat to find her way to the Ledge. Wind Westwardly.

Note 7th. This day at home till 9 p.m. when Horatio, Abner and myself bid farewell to our friends and waded to the Ledge, when after a long time and much trouble hailing, launching Boat etc., we got on board the vessel at 1 a.m. on

Saturday. Very cold. Wind North.

Note 8th. All things ready at 5 a.m. weighed anchor and sailed down the River, passed Saint Andrews at Sunrising, and went out through Latete (sic) passage, thence sailed down the American Coast. Crew, consisting of myself, Wm. Harper, mate, John Paul, John Earl, David Conally, seamen, Jos Irvin, cook, Horatio Hill, Abner McAllister and Reuben Whitney.

9th. Sunday. No land in sight. Weather moderating, wind Light, snow. Corked in Bow port. 67° 10W.

10th. Very thick snow storm. Ship *Elizabeth* from Saint Andrews passed us. Wind E. N.E. 66° 16.

11th. Sleet and snow at intervals. Wind inclining to the Southward 65° 11 W. Lat. by Obs 40° 09N.

12th. Weather moderate and wind light at E. by S. 64° 15 W. Lat 38° 25 N.

13th. This day a very strong gale from Northwest with a tremendous sea. Send the Brig S.E. as near as we could. She requires nearly one quarter of the compass to steer her in. Lat. 37° 05 W. L 62° 18.

14th. Weather more moderate. Employed myself reading newspapers, writing, etc. 61° 18 Lat. 35° 03 N.

15th. This day the wind increased to a gale, lay the vessel to at ten a.m. Wind S.E. changed to S.W. 60° 123.

16th. Sunday. A very severe gale, still continues laying to. The sea running tremendous high, causes the vessel to strain and make much water; pump constantly going. In the afternoon wind moderates a little and we attempted to send her – the wind increasing again to its former violence blew the foresail to pieces. Lay to again. Shipped a great quantity of water over the rail, and expected for a time that she would sweep everything from the Deck. The sea broke the foreward deck load Stancheon, and two tiers of the shingles about half the way were lost. The day spent between hope and fear – a hope that we might survive the storm, and a fear that some of those dreadful seas might sweep us into oblivion. Long. 59° 00.

17th. The gale still continues. The vessel laying to under a close reefed main topsail (throughout the gale). In the latter part of the day it began to moderate. Everything completely drenched in water from forward to aft, not a corner but what the sea and rain has broke into – wind West, 58° 00.

18th. The wind is light and variable attended with squalls of rain and sunshine at intervals. We made sail again after a gale of seventy hours, the longest that ever I experienced at sea, and I don't know but what the strongest, as I never saw a vessel roll her lower yards so near the water as at this time, when they were not more than five or six feet above it, and the water about three feet on the lee rail. No weather to dry any clothes therefore everything continues wet, beds not excepted. This scene would not compare well with the privileges and enjoyments at home especially that of a Sunday. As a boy says "if he were as sick at home as here he should be in bed," while here he cannot even remain in bed when permitted. Wind west southwardly – Long. 57° 30. Lat. 33°37 West.

19th. Weather very unsettled. At noon in a very heavy squall of wind and rain, the wheel unshipt, the vessel brought too parted the Foot Rope of the Fore top sail, and blew it to pieces. Everything on board continues wet from constant rain and spray. Wind West Southwesterly. Long. 56°50 Lat. 32° 10.

20th. At 8 a.m. bent a new Fore Top sail. The weather appearing a little more settled. A strong breeze to the Southward and Westward. Finest day since leaving Saint Andrews but cool for the Latitude. Some rain squalls in the afternoon. Wind West. Lat 31° 39N Long 56° 42 W.

21st. Weather unsettled, and wind variable inclining

to the Southward. Long 56° 42 W.

22nd. Weather fine affording an opportunity for the first time of drying our clothes and of performing the duties of the vessel, in refitting and repairing damages sustained in the late gale and in the frosty weather. Wind WSW. Lat. 27° 58N Long 55° 50W.

23rd. Sunday. Very pleasant and the air clear and salubrious. Wind Southwest. Lat. 26° 339 long. 55° 08W.

24th. Wind getting very light and weather fine. Employed myself fitting a Harpoon. People employed repairing a Topsail. Wind West Southwardly. Lat. 25°36. Long 54° 30W.

25th. Calm first part of the day with a long rolling sea. Wrought upon a sail part of this day and attended to the duties of the vessel devolving on me. Reading, etc. West lat. 24° 38. Long 54° 30W

26th. Weather fine and wind variable. A Boil on my wrist a troublesome companion. Overhauled our stock of bread and moved it, to get it out of the way of rats. 22° 29 Long. 54° 00.

27th. This day crossed the Northern Tropic and got the first East or Trade wind. Wrist continues very painful. A sail in sight. Lat. 234 1N. Long. 54° 10W – at Noon.

28th. Light airs. A ship still in sight. Steering about SSW. Lamp Oil spilled which obliges us to steer by moon light, repairing old sails. Lat. 22° 19N Long. 54° 25W.

29th. A strong breeze, the vessel under full sail, corking and repairing Armstrong's boat, she being in very bad order.

30th. Sunday. Weather very fine. Read in the Bible the Books of Prophets Daniel, Amos and Joel. Attended to the necessary duties of the vessel. Lat 18° 48 Long 55° 20.

31st. Last day of January, the sea smooth and sky clear. Cut out a pair of canvas trousers for Horatio H. Overhauled the canvas and found that we had expended altogether since we left Halifax, 3 bolts of Brown and 1 Bleached, leaving 3 Bleached out of 7 bought in Halifax. Lat. 17° 02 Long.55° 50W.

It was February 4 when the Captain and crew of the *Keziah* finally saw land for the first time in more than a month since leaving home. His journal continues.

Note Feb. 4th Wind light and variable, very warm, I suppose 86° of the Thermometer. At noon saw the land about twenty-five miles distant. 3 p.m. an entire calm, Barbados bearing WbyN. Put small boat out and washed myself, and made preparations for going ashore.

Once on shore Capt. McAllister began his second role, that of salesman for the cargo he carried. It is ironic to note that, "the more things change the more they remain the same." He went on shore and found that, although lumber was needed in Barbados, the buyers were reluctant and observed that "people run of an idea they will get Boards for nothing almost of the Americans as well as every other thing, and I cannot but say that their expectations may be realized in a measure, as they are crowding in for the first market."

Also noted at the time was his observation of three newly arrived lumber vessels which received "much damage" in the gale of the 15th and 16th.

Capt. McAllister left them to their haggling in Barbados and "steered for Tobago to take the Islands in course" where he would eventually sell his cargo, pick up return shipments of molasses and sugar before arriving back in Halifax on May 9 ...in yet another storm.

"The wind came on to blow hard at S.E. at 8 in the evening with a very thick fog and rain, when we hauled off the coast and carried on whole Topsails at the risque of carrying away sails and yard to gain an offing as the wind was dead on shore. At 5 A.M. the wind abating hauled in for the land. At noon saw the land, and in company with several small vessels got into the harbour at 5 P.M. although the fog continued to veil the land at any great distance.

"Had a pilot on board 2 hours. Came to an anchor, passengers went ashore. Sounded several times in the morning and caught two Codfish. Saw large shoals of Fish."

On May 10 Captain McAllister would go to the customs house and begin the business of docking in Halifax and selling his cargo of sugar and molasses and, incidentally, ordering the Mate to resign his office after going back to the ship and finding him "about half seas over and very little doing."

A further note indicated that "the sailors were of little use while lying at the wharf after visiting the grog shops."

One tends perhaps to sympathize with those sailors after such a voyage!

Miracle on the 28th Parallel

Captain Bradshaw arrived at Saint John on August 2 1844 at the helm of the schooner *Herold*, bringing with him a strange story of what should still be considered a most miraculous survival.

The *Herold* had left Boston in July enroute to Saint John when the skipper noticed a Brigantine of about 200 tons abandoned and lying on her beam ends, nearly full of water. He noted in his log book that it was July 19 and that he was at a latitude of 28°-40° N. and 72°-30° west at the time.

The Schooner *Washington* from New York was lying near and, it being very calm, the crews of both vessels boarded the Brig and cut a hole through her bow bulwarks.

Then, as today, abandoned vessels were fair game on the high seas. If they, or any of their cargo, could be salvaged it was "finders keepers" all the way. What the crews of the *Herold* and the *Washington* found was not what they expected!

There, in the fo'c'sle, after they cut through the bow was a little boy believed to be about 12 years of age. He was sitting on the head of a water cask with his feet in the water but with an abundance of provisions nearby.

As soon as he saw daylight he began to sing merrily and was promptly taken aboard the *Herold* to be cared for until the schooner reached Saint John.

The Brig's log was rescued but, while it stated that the boy was from Jamaica, there was no indication of the date when the bad weather struck that capsized the ship, resulting in the boy being washed into the forecastle and attaining his precarious perch in the wet darkness.

The boy supposed that the crew had perished but he had no idea who the captain was or what was the name of the vessel.

A bit of research brought to light the fact that a lifeboat had been picked up at sea on July 11 carrying the captain and the crew of the Brig *Sir Leonard Smith*, sailing from New York to Kingston, Jamaica. The vessel was capsized and abandoned on the night of July 10 and a boy was said to have drowned in the wreck.

Captain Bradshaw's diary noted that "the poor little fellow must have been in his gloomy and lonesome confinement for nine days."

Eventually the boy was sent back home to Jamaica where his grandchildren no doubt heard the story of his miraculous escape from death on the high seas. The chronicle of this story did not indicate any name for the boy.

The *Herold*, a 55 ton schooner, was built in St. Martins by the Bradshaw and Vail builders in 1834. She continued to ply her trade between Saint John and Boston until April 11, 1852 when she was lost in a gale enroute to Boston. Both her crew and her cargo, containing 200 barrels of Alewives and 25,000 feet of lumber, survived the storm and the salvage was claimed by fishermen from Cape Elizabeth, Maine.

For the Good of His Health?

Young William Logan of Saint John was a passenger on the *Alexander McKenzie* when she set sail from Saint John in the winter of 1876 with Captain Harvey Copp of Waterside, Albert County at the helm. Young William's father, also William Logan, was a part owner of the vessel.

As was a custom of the time young William was sent to sea "for the good of his health."

Accommodations on the *Alexander McKenzie* were quite luxurious, boasting of bathrooms and "being fitted with all modern conveniences."

Built by James E. Black of St. Martins and launched from Parks Ship Yard on Nov. 10, 1875, the vessel was iron kneed and copper fastened up to 21 feet and there was "more pitch pine in her construction than is usual in vessels of her class. She had a half-poop and house and her cabins were nicely finished," according to Frederick Cochrane, Saint John ship historian of the early 20th century.

"She was a handsome looking vessel with 181 feet over all, a 36 foot beam and 22 foot hold."

Not only was she elegant but she was fast. On her maiden voyage December 15, 1875 she cleared Saint John for Liverpool with a cargo of deals shipped by George McKean and made the passage in 22 days!

Not long after that, on March 10, 1876 with young William aboard she was bound from Pensacola for Liverpool with a cargo of hard pine timber when, about north of the Azores during a heavy gale while reefing the fore-upper topsail, an ordinary seaman fell from aloft and struck on the starboard chain locker. He was picked up in an unconscious state remaining that way for seven days until the vessel arrived at Liverpool and he was sent to hospital.

The *Alexander McKenzie* unloaded her cargo and began the next step of its voyage when, about midway up the mouth of St. George's channel the ship stood in to make the land.

"It was blowing strong from the southwest. Just after daylight on March 30 Captain Copp ordered the mate to put the anchors on the rails and, in order to do so, he was obliged to take the jib sheet and belay it to the port windlass bit. After the anchor was put on the rain a sailor took jib sheet back where it belonged."

William Logan was on the forecastle head at the time. The sheet struck him and knocked him overboard at the port cat-head. The cry of "man overboard" was raised and young Logan drifted along the ship's side. The man at the wheel threw him the end of the lee main brace which he caught but, owing to the ship going through the water at the rate of six miles per hour, he was unable to hold on.

In the meantime Captain Copp came up on deck and called out to him to catch the log line, which he did. The line slipped through his fingers until he came to the log where he held on.

In the meantime the ship was shaking in the wind and the main yards were hauled back all the way and taken off the ship. They hauled in on the log and Logan, for all that his health was questionable, gamely hung on.

One of the seamen, with a bowline around him, was lowered over the stern of the ship with another bowline attached to him, all ready to put around Logan when he got hold of him. As he got close to Logan he made a grab for his coat collar but only managed to catch him by the shoulder.

The sea was heavy and lifted the ship's stern out of the water, the seaman then lost his grip on Logan who promptly disappeared under the water.

Determined to get the young man back on board one of the ships boats was lowered and several of the crew spent nearly five hours looking for the luckless fellow.

Young William Logan was never found and the *Alexander McKenzie* squared away for Liverpool again, the Union Jack hoisted at half mast in the Mizzen rigging.

Three years later, on December 15, 1879 the *Alexander McKenzie* carrying a cargo of case oil bound from New York for Dunkirk, France caught fire in the North Sea and burned to the water's edge. The ship was lost but the crew fared better than young William had on that first voyage … they were saved.

A Foggy Night in the Reversing Falls and a Ferry Boat ride to remember!

The Reversing Falls, where the St. John River meets the high tides of the Bay of Fundy causes the river to flow rapidly downstream at times, tumbling over large rocks and dropping several feet before joining the outgoing tide. At other times the flow dramatically reverses and the Bay of Fundy's incoming tide causes a similar tumbling and drop as it pushes its way into the river.

Only when the tide is "slack," neither high nor low, is the river placid at the gorge, allowing vessels to sail peacefully either up-or-down river.

Needless to say there are many stories of mysterious creatures, sunken ships and lost treasures told about the Reversing Falls. Even Paul Bunyan has a role to play, along with Glooscap, in the mythology of their creation and their impact on the history of the river and surrounding area.

Even after the Reversing Falls were successfully bridged a crossing point above the gorge, at "Indiantown," (in Portland an area later to become the "north end" of the City of Saint John) to Pleasant Point, was in regular use as a crossing by small vessels. Eventually a ferry boat system was established at the site.

Two days before Christmas in 1872 a smaller ferry continued to transport people across the river in deep fog after the regular ferry had finished its run for the night. On board were a woman, a boy and thirteen men.

The ferry had no sooner left Indiantown than a strong down river wind came up. This, coupled with the fact that the tide was going out in the Bay of Fundy, drawing the river water with it and causing a cold mist to rise from the water resulted in a suddenly more dangerous trip than usual. One of the men remarked that he believed the boat was moving down stream and that the water was becoming more rough than usual. The ferryman brushed off the suggestion, assuring the passengers that all was under control and they were in no danger. But there were those who noticed he was pulling his oars with increased vigour.

Nevertheless the passengers were satisfied, believing this increased activity was taking them closer to the far shore when in reality they were just entering the centre of the channel. The wind increased and suddenly everyone realized they were, indeed rapidly heading down stream and in imminent danger of "going over the falls."

They urged the ferryman to turn back but it was too late. Everyone realized the danger would only be increased if there was any attempt made to turn so the ferryman continued his now frantic rowing forward while, at the same time, trying to calm the near hysterical passengers, assuring them they were getting nearer their destination.

One passenger, out of his mind from a combination of fear and alcohol, said he could manage the boat and seized one of the oars. In spite of the protests of the ferryman and the passengers he began frantically plying the oar without any sense of coordination as a result the boat soon became unmanageable and it was impossible to tell in what direction it was heading.

At the same moment a new horror was added to the scene as the roar of the falls filled the air above the noise of the wind. The thunderous reverberation of thousands of tons of water rushing over the falls fell like a death knell upon the ears of the now silence-stricken passengers.

There was not one who did not feel doomed to meet their maker within seconds as they were swept into the seething and boiling water ahead.

The silence amid the thunder of the falls was replaced by cries of terror and shrieks of prayer.

The rowing stopped, they could see nothing but the reflection of their own terror then suddenly the boat struck against something hard that held it for a timeless moment.

The passengers near the bow sprang forward and grasped a projecting rock. It was a part of Goat Island, no more than a boat length away from the falls. In moments they were out of the boat, safe for the time being from almost certain death.

Their situation was still a serious one. The night was terribly cold and they were surrounded by dense fog. The roar of the falls precluded any possibility of their cries for help being heard either from shore or from the suspension bridge which crossed the falls at that time.

Here they remained for two hours that seemed more like twenty. At last the fog lifted, the tide turned and rose enough for them to stem the current of the river and pull away from the island to their destination of Pleasant Point.

In 1859 Robert Foulis' Foghorn let sailors see with their ears

Until 1859 captains sailing their vessels around the world had only bell buoys to guide them through treacherous seas, not the least treacherous of which was the Bay of Fundy.

Robert Foulis, a man who had studied both engineering and surgery and received recognition as a talented artist in his native Scotland, had a bad experience in the murky fog of the Bay of Fundy after coming to New Brunswick. The feeling of helplessness that experience engendered stayed with him until, in 1854, he conceived the idea of constructing a steam fog horn.

For several years he had been advocating the construction of a good alarm, operated by steam, which would automatically permit compressed steam to escape at given intervals through a horn – large enough to carry the sound many miles across the water.

During that time a friend of Foulis' obtained the plans and had the fog horn constructed on Partridge Island in 1859. In the meantime a shrewd businessman took the plans and patented them, enjoying rich rewards over the years as countries around the world adopted the Foulis style fog horn.

The first Foulis fog horn served Partridge Island

faithfully until 1906 when it was replaced with a similar system until 1931, when a semideisel engine replaced the steam and a long column replaced the horn. This resulted in a much louder and far reaching blast caused by rapid air vibration through the column.

At this writing, in July of 1998, the *Letters to the Editor* of the *Times Globe* are filled with protest from small ship and fishing vessel owners bewailing the discontinuance of the Fundy Fog Horn on Partridge Island ... a sound New Brunswick mariners have long depended on to guide them safely through the mists and fog at the entrance to Saint John Harbour. Electronic virtual reality doesn't quite have the same, comforting sound as that familiar "Oooh ... Ahhh" of old.

Legacies of the Sea

New Brunswick Sea Stories

Pillars of the Community got rich from whales

Among the fascinating legacies of the late Frederick Cochrane is the story of the whaling business operated out of the Port of Saint John late in the 19th Century. It was a lucrative business indeed, one in which no fewer that 150 city residents were partners back in 1837. Among them were men whose names are still remembered today for the role they played in making Saint John the bustling and booming city at that time.

Ironically the tempers of many of those men, if they were alive today, would no doubt see them directed against the wholesale slaughter of whales. It is difficult to relate the city's most prestigious cabinet-maker ... a craftsman whose sideboards and dining tables, chairs and sofas are treasured today as works of art ... to the role of entrepreneur in such an industry. Yet none other than John Nisbet was president of the St. John Mechanics Whale Fishing Company when it was incorporated the day after Christmas, December 26, 1837.

Furthermore, the secretary of the corporation, one John Kirby, swore before H. Porter, Justice of the Peace for the City and County of Saint John, that the members of such corporation were bona fide British subjects and that "no Foreigner or Alien hath any share or interest in the stock of this said company."

Other well known residents among the membership

included Henry Chubb of Chubb's Corner fame, Thomas Barlow Jr.; Ewen Cameron, Edward Drury, Robert Foulis (whose place in history is tied to his invention of the fog-horn); Thomas Heans, Isaac Jewett, Hugh Mackay (a name closely tied to politics as well as the stock market i.e. Pitfield Mackay longtime stock brokers of Saint John), Alexander McMillan of McMillan Press, David J. Merritt (Merritt house is better known today as Saint John's "Loyalist House.")

The whaling industry reaped profits from the very beginning, on May 11, 1841 the St. John company declared a 20 per cent profit and a 14 per cent profit the next year which amounted to 20 shillings a share. It was considered to be in a "prosperous condition" at the time.

Among the ships in their fleet were the *Java*, 419 tons, built by W.& R. Wright at Courtenay Bay in 1839; the *Royal William*, 277 tons purchased by the company but built in England in 1831; *the Pacific*, 347 tons and the *Mechanic*[1] were built in Carleton (West Saint John) by Messers. Olive in 1837.

James Millidge also owned and operated three whaling ships the Thomas Millidge, Peruvian and the Mozambique.[2]

According to Cochrane, in those days Water Street below Duke Street was not regarded as a public thorough-fare. At times it was lined on either side with casks of whale oil to the extent that, through its entire length, there was "barely room for the passage of a single cart."

Most of the whaling vessels were under the command of English and American captains but their crews were made up from New Brunswickers. The crew was paid in shares.

Whalers were square rigged and it took a crew of 30 to 35 men to outfit one ship. When they left their home port each vessel carried its own supply of casks which were filled with water for ballast, until replaced with whale oil during the voyage.

An indication of the amount of cargo the whalers carried can best be realized from the following statistics. The *James Stewart* arrived in St. John on April 2, 1835 carrying 1,270 bbls of black oil, 530bbls of sperm oil and 20,000lbs. of whale bone.[3]

Practical jokes were the order of the day along the waterfront then, as now, wherever men labour long and hard with their hands. On one such occasion Dr. Abraham Gesner, of kerosene fame and founder of the New Brunswick Museum (the first in Canada) was the butt of some rather earthy humour. Gesner's discovery of the jawbone of a Mastodon in Albert County (see display in the New Brunswick Museum) prompted much jeering as the whalers suggested the jawbone was nothing more than whalebone which found its way into ladies' corsets. No doubt the threat of kerosene to the whaling industry prompted much of their derision.

On June 4, 1932 Cochrane wrote that the passing of the whaling industry was directly related to the discovery of petroleum fuels which ushered in the period of electric lights and telephones.

By May of 1845 newspapers were beginning to editorialize on the waste and wantonness of whaling, deploring the sacrifice of these magnificent creatures for the sake of some oil for lamps and whalebone for ladies' corsets.[4]

---

[1] Fifth vessel built in NB for the whaling trade. See story *Stewart the Whaler,* in *St. John Courier*, May 28, 1836.
[2] *St. John Courier*, July 30, 1836.
[3] Page 9 Cochrane notes description of homecoming of a whaler.
[4] May 13 1845, *St. John Courier.*

Leprosy in New Brunswick

I can vaguely remember as a child hearing stories about a 'leper colony' in New Brunswick. It is all rather vague in my mind ... mixed up with Bible stories and Jesus daring to touch a leper. In later years the horrors of the disease were diminished somewhat as successful research gradually eliminated the disturbing image of leprosy. Over time, leprosy simply disappeared from our awareness.

Recently all those references from my childhood came streaming back into my consciousness with the reading of an excellent series of articles by Harold W.J. Adams in the *Miramichi Leader.*

Harold is an insatiable historian who has delved into the history of the people of the Miramichi with great fervour. I had the pleasure of meeting and talking with him while doing my own research for this book in the Miramichi area. As a consequence, I discovered the intriguing story of how leprosy may have imposed its dreadful presence on New Brunswick as the result of a shipwreck back in 1880.

No matter what version of the story you read or hear, the bottom line is that the disease reached here through someone who arrived in the Miramichi area by ship some time in the mid-eighteenth century.

An article titled *The Strange and Tragic History of the Lazaretto at Tracadie, NB* which appeared in the Saint John

newspaper *The Daily Telegraph* on July 20, 1880, reprinted from *The New York World,* provided the following explanation.

In 1758 the *Indienne*, a French vessel which had been engaged in the Levant trade ran aground at the mouth of the Miramichi River.

She was laden with a general cargo of considerable value.

The fishermen of the neighbourhood came to the rescue and worked hard to save the ship but, in a few days, she broke up and went to pieces.

It was in the fall and the gales which sweep the Gulf of St. Lawrence at this season of the year breached her hard and fast and then "tore her asunder."

The captain had no money to pay the fishermen, for this was the time of the Acadian troubles when French vessels were dogged by English frigates, but he gave the fishermen several bundles of second hand clothing which he had shipped from Smyrna.

The fishermen were very hospitable, took the crew into their homes and provided for them until they obtained passage to the port of Morlaix, France from which port they had sailed.

With the wearing of the old clothes and the consorting with the ship's hands, some of whom were "Lascars" the natives of this district contracted Leprosy.

The disease broke out in the spring of 1759. The town of Beaubair was dreadfully stricken: 800 persons, or over two-thirds of the population, died and were put underground for the living were unable to give them a Christian burial.

At Point Beaubair the intendant, or government agent after whom the town was named, was among the first victims.

The survivors, many of them carrying the infection,

fled. Some to Miramichi and others to Prince Edward Island but the majority went to Caraquet, Pokemouche and Tracadie.

Beaubair, or Beaubere as he signed himself, was buried on a small island outside Newcastle, which the Acadians called, "Ille du Gentilhomme Lepreaux – the Island of the Leprous Gentleman."

There was no authentic record of the disease for the next fifty years, Miramichi and the coast line from Shippagan, at the entrance of the Baie des Chaleurs to Cape Tormentine, were little known save to the local fishermen and an occasional lumber craft.

The New World story speaks of the "Levant trade" and it should be noted that "Levant" was used to describe countries of the eastern Mediterranean.

It may also be read as "East or Orient." The expression "Lascar" has a Hindi meaning of East Indian sailor.

Smyrna was an ancient city in Asia Minor now called Ismir, Turkey. The word Indienne is the feminine of Indien, meaning to be seasoned as with curry in the East Indian style.

Adams' research suggests that if leprosy came to New Brunswick via the L'Indienne de Morlais, it would be important to realize the history of the area surrounding Morlais, France for in the district of Madeleine there was established a legal leper colony.

He goes on to note that the 1832 work, *A Compendius History of the Province of New Brunswick and the District of Gaspe in Lower Canada*, Robert Cooney writes:

"It is said the disease, thus superinduced by their impoverished condition, was communicated by the *L'Indienne of Morlaix,* a vessel wrecked near the entrance of the harbour, and whose remains are still lying a short distance from the mouth of Baie des Vents River."

In 1979 the Anglican Church women of Bay du Vin

their work titled, *Looking Back: A history of Bay du Vin, New Brunswick* attributes the *L'Indienne de Morlaix* for the community's name.

"The French were bringing in casks of wine, presumably for sale to the early settlers of this area. They were proceeding successfully until the English were gaining on them and were very likely to seize the load.

"To prevent this, the French threw the casks of wine into what is now the inner Bay du Vin Bay, which means "Bay of Wine" in French ....

" ......Some credence is given to this legend by the fact that a ship was indeed sunk at the mouth of the Bay du Vin River. It was reputedly a French Man of War, named *L'Indienne of Morlaix.*"

There are, of course, a variety of stories concerning the advent of Leprosy on the Miramichi. Most of them have a tie-in to the sea, which is logical when one considers that the seas were the highways of the time and, like today, people carried disease with them as they passed from port to port and country to country.

Much to my surprise I learned that Leprosy is far from cured, although it is more controlled and research continues. The following information taken from *Groliers 1997 Multimedia Encyclopedia* is most enlightening ... albeit still disturbing.

Once a disease so dreaded that its victims were isolated in so-called leper colonies, leprosy can now be controlled and its resulting disfigurements prevented. The infectious agent, Mycobacterium leprae, is a bacillus in the same family as the one that causes tuberculosis. (It was discovered in 1874 by a Norwegian physician, Gerhard Hansen, and leprosy is sometimes called Hansen's Disease.) The agent is thought to be transmitted by skin-to-skin contact and nasal discharges. About 95 per cent of the persons exposed to the bacterium are immune, however, so leprosy is not considered highly contagious. Because the bacterium is very slow growing, the incubation period can range from one to thirty years, but the average is about three to five years. The organism invades the peripheral nerves, skin, and mucous membranes, damaging the nerves and causing anaesthesia. The resulting insensitivity can lead to unnoticed and therefore neglected injuries: this accounts for many of the deformities--such as loss of fingers--that occur in leprosy. Paralysis may also result; in advanced cases, numbness of the eyes may lead to blindness through trauma or infection.

Forms of Leprosy

Two main forms of the disease are known: tuberculoid and lepromatous. The tuberculoid form mainly involves the skin and nerves. Plaques--such as a red, raised rim surrounding a pale, flat centre— occur most often on the arms and legs. Nerves under the plaques are damaged, and the areas become numb: contraction and wasting of muscles often occur. The lepromatous form is a more generalized infection that involves skin, mouth, nasal passages, upper respiratory tract, eyes, nerves, adrenal glands, and testicles. Various skin eruptions may cover the entire body, but numbness is more patchy and less severe than in tuberculoid leprosy. In advanced stages, however, lepromatous leprosy can cause ulcers, eyebrow loss, collapse of the nose, enlarged ear lobes and facial features, and blindness.

Treatment

The main drug used to treat leprosy is dapsone. In the 1960s, however, dapsone-resistant cases began to appear, and today the drug is usually given with other bactericidal drugs such as rifampine. Clofazimine, approved for U.S. use in 1987 against lepromatous leprosy, is also usually given in combination with other drugs. Thalidomide, made infamous in the 1960s for its teratogenic effects, has been found to reduce fever, skin lesions, and pain in certain patients. Leprosy vaccines, the product of cloning techniques as well as more traditional methods, are being developed and are undergoing clinical trials.

Leprosy is still with us

The World Health Organization has an internet site on the World Wide Web on the topic of leprosy.

It says since ancient times leprosy has been regarded by the community as a contagious, mutilating and incurable disease. There are many countries in Asia, Africa and Latin America with a significant number of leprosy cases.

As of 1995 around two point four million people live in countries where the prevalence of leprosy is more than one case per ten thousand population. It is estimated that in 1995 there were between one and two million people visibly and irreversibly disabled due to past and present leprosy who require to be cared for by the community in which they live.

The WHO estimated that about two million cases of leprosy exist in South-East Asia, Africa and the Americas. Among them one point three million are registered for treatment, of whom one million are treated with multidrug therapy. The number of new cases detected world wide each year is about half a million.

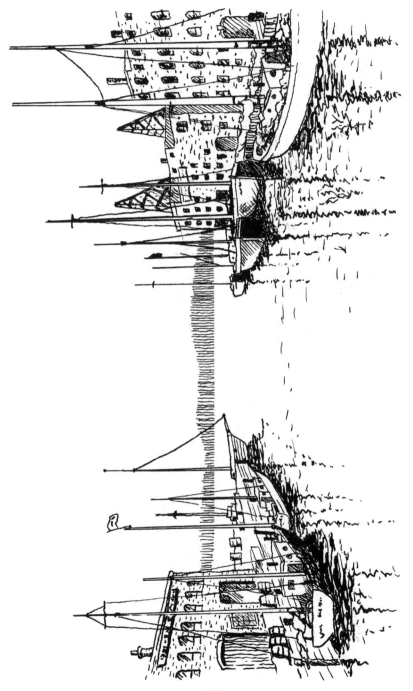

How to build a wooden ship ...
New Brunswick Style

The shipbuilding boom of the mid-nineteenth century touched the entire coast of New Brunswick: from Bathurst, Richibucto and Shippagan in the north to St. Martins, Saint John and St. Andrews in the south and in numerous communities in between.

Without a doubt Saint John was put on the maritime map through its reputation for building the fastest ship in the world as the *Marco Polo* continued to prove. Other fast and sturdy vessels came off the ways almost daily.

It was not uncommon to see six or seven hundred men crossing the Marsh Creek bridge as they walked to work in the shipyards, six days a week. They were building splendid specimens of marine architecture that would carry the then plentiful supplies of New Brunswick timber to British markets, where both the lumber and the ships that brought it would find a ready sale.

The rapidity with which they built these ships was marvellous to behold. The keel, comprised of high quality sticks of birch would be carefully put in place in the stocks. Then the stern and bow posts would be fitted in.

In a few days the framers, working in two gangs one on either side of the ship, would be engaged in putting the frames together and hoisting them up into position.

Within the space of a few weeks most of the framework of the vessel would be in place. It took a bit more time

101

to fit in the fore and aft sections. At this point the ship was just a skeleton, a framework on which to place the next addition, her planking.

The plankers, like the framers, worked in two gangs, one on each side of the ship. The top sides were planked first, then the men would hit a faster pace. A yard gang would ready the planks in a steam box: the planking gang would carry them up and put them on. The hole-borers would already be boring with wonderful accuracy, then the bolt drivers and tree nail drivers would come along to complete this phase. The music of their work was a pleasure to the ears of anyone connected with the sea.

Caulkers, caulking the seams and dubbers dubbing off the rough spots to make good lines would join the chorus of the shipyard din and rattle.

In a short time the ship would be all caulked and sealed. The great iron knees would be put in to strengthen the ship. The deck would go on. The houses, fore and aft, and the cabins would be finished in fine style by the joiners.

Next came the masts with the spar makers putting the tremendous timbers in place. Sometimes the masts were put in position after the ship was launched. Once the masts were in place the painters literally swarmed over the ship. When they were finished she was ready for launching.

Launching days, then as now, were days of celebration. Men from the other shipyards would gather with their sledges to help knock the props out and send the ship into the water. Cheers would go up as the latest addition to the fleet of New Brunswick vessels sailing the seven seas would slide down the ways.

While the vessel would generally leave the ways with ease the exercise would nearly always be accompanied by great clouds of smoke and, occasionally, flames would burst forth caused by the friction on the greased ways.

One vessel, listing badly in the stocks due to an earthquake tremor, is said to have slid down the ways on her side.

A tugboat was always waiting to take the newly launched ship to her berth at the wharf where she would then be fitted out for sea.

It was not uncommon to see as many as four ships in a yard at one time, and a total of seventeen or eighteen ships under construction in the stocks of all the yards together.

Shipbuilding was the lifeblood of Saint John and the skills of those block makers, sail makers and chandlers have been handed down for generations, albeit changed to meet the demands of modern needs. They carry with them a natural instinct and pride in the honourable trade of shipbuilding.

New Brunswick Sea Stories

Shipwrecks

New Brunswick Sea Stories

The wreck of the Humacao becomes a tomb

One of the most rewarding aspects of writing stories relating to true events in our history, is the interest individuals throughout the province take in contributing to these collections. Blair E. Bartlett of Saint John is one such person.

Mr. Bartlett wrote:

"Seeing that you are planning to write a book on shipwrecks, I have enclosed an August 1886 newspaper article entitled *Eleven Lives Lost* . My great-great Grandfather, Bartholomew Armstrong and my Great, great grandmother's first cousin, T. Hartley Stackhouse were among those who drowned. Perhaps you may ...... want to include it in your next book."

It is indeed a fascinating story and I thank Mr. Bartlett for sharing it with us.

The story was subtitled numerous times with statements like, Excitement in St. John and Portland; The Worst Catastrophe in Years ... Nearly all Married Men Who Lose Their Lives. And those subtitles only begin to suggest the depth of the story.

A 1,650 ton Spanish steamer named the Humacao was on the passage between Baltimore and St. John (sic) carrying a crew of about 40 men when it went aground on Wallace Rock on the Murr Ledges of Grand Manan during a thick fog on August 5, 1886. Since there was a light sea running at the time the Captain and the crew decided to stay on board until assistance could be summoned from Grand Manan, about five miles distant.

However, during the day the sea rose and, fearing the vessel would break up, the Captain and crew left her and went ashore. The captain eventually set out for St. John which he reached the following Friday evening.

According to the news report, old navigators of the bay regarded the Murr Ledges as among the most dangerous rocks on the New Brunswick coast.

"Far distant from the mainland of Grand Manan, they are exposed to the full force of every gale that blows."

As a result the position of the wreck was considered very dangerous. When the agent of the underwriters visited the scene, and then invited tenders for raising the steamer, no one could be found willing to take the risk involved.

Apparently there was one chance that might be successful. Since the steamer was stranded on the inner of the four rocks, slightly protected from the seas by the other rocks when coming from Wallace Ledges, access to the steamer might be achieved at high tide. Although, even then, it would be difficult to access the Humacao because at tide her decks were within a few feet of the water level. To add to the problem, in a high wind the sea would rise to such an extent that the waves would wash over the decks entirely.

Nevertheless some men, including Donald McNeil of New York and James Griffiths from Saint John bought the wreck and set out from Saint John on a Saturday night in the tug Dirigo with a crew of ten men. On the Monday evening the tug returned to Saint John and it was reported the breaking up of the wreck was under way.

A short time later Mr. J.H. Harding, marine fisheries

department agent in Saint John, received a telegram from Mr. McLaughlin, the lighthouse keeper at Southwest Head, Grand Manan. He advised that the steamer Humacao was breaking up. Her smokestack and foremast had already gone by the board and, although a long distance away, he said he could distinctly see with a glass that the effects of the heavy gale of the previous evening had made "an impression" on the wreck. He further predicted that those on board were in a position of "extreme peril," adding that although the sun was shining brightly the heavy sea was still running.

Mr. Harding posted the telegraph in the Board of Trade rooms and women and children of the men hired to break up the wreck waited in dread for further news of their loved ones.

A second despatch was received around two o'clock in the afternoon. It was from Captain Johnson and contained the following words: "Steamship hove off the ledge and sunk; all hands supposed to have been lost."

The despatch was from Seal Cove and addressed to a Mr. H.J. Olive who posted it immediately and panic erupted in the streets. The Board of Trade office was besieged with inquiries for further particulars. Telegrams were sent to every conceivable place in Grand Manan but no details were forthcoming save to say that on the Tuesday evening when the weather got "thick" the Dirigo, which was harboured at Seal Cove, ran out to the ledge and asked the men on board the wreck to go ashore. They declined. Determined to stay by the wreck during the night.

A special to the *Telegraph* from Southwest Head said that on Wednesday morning "the main mast and bridge went by the board at noon when the ship submerged. I could see the men on the bridge a short time before the vessel went under. There were twelve men on board. All were lost but one, the young lad Daly who was saved by the tug at 5 p.m."

The *Telegraph* story included the following names:

James Griffiths, one of the nine men who purchased the steamer for salvage. He has a wife but no family. He belongs to St. John, and is well and favourably known.

James Napier of Portland, who was foreman of the gang of workmen. He has a wife and five children.

Robert Johnson of Portland, carpenter, who was at one time a policeman on the St. John force. He has a wife and grown up family.

James Strayhorn of Portland, caulker, who has a wife and one child.

James Clarke of Portland, who has a wife and four or five children.

Hartley Stackhouse, son of Richard Stackhouse of Portland; has a wife and five children.

Alexander Scribner of Portland; has a wife and two children.

Jeremiah Daley, a son of James Daley, cartman.

Two names of the missing and presumed drowned were missing from the list.

One cannot help but wonder what hardship the surviving family members must have endured in an era when men were the breadwinners and women, unless well educated, had little recourse to employment other than housework or washerwomen. While the churches would do what they could the families would undoubtedly be practically destitute.

(Portland, refers to that part of the city north of Saint John which was not yet amalgamated with that city.)

Bottles on the bottom too often become a diver's trophy

Hundreds of years ago smuggling was a regular business carried on in the Bay of Fundy as enterprising colonists brought with them the profitable practices enjoyed by many fishing vessels in the English Channel.

The favourite landing places were around the flat, isolated spots along the coast. The cargo, then as now, was New England rum and tobacco. The smugglers' boats would run in under cover of darkness and, if they received word that the customs men were on the lookout, they would bury the barrels of spirits in the sand and store the tobacco in caves and crevices among the rocks until a safe opportunity was afforded to bring them inland.

The old-time "tidewaiters," as the Custom House officers were called, had many interesting stories to relate of their weary watches in open boats on dark and often stormy nights ... and of hand-to-hand combats with the smugglers who often showed fight in defence of their goods.

When word was received at Customs, through very secret and private channels, that a landing would be attempted at a certain designated place several of the tidewaiters would embark on one of their fast revenue cutters and cruise along the shore, generally at night, and lie in wait to intercept the landing.

A short item from a Saint John newspaper of 1842

gives a decription of one such exciting event in the life of the old time customs men of New Brunswick.

"On Sunday night last a party of Her Majesty's Officers of Customs went to the Straight Shore in the Parish of Portland where they found five barrels of smuggled liquor. The smugglers had fled at the approach of the revenue men who took possession of the casks, secured a horse and sled and, at an early hour in the morning, proceeded with their catch towards the Custom House in the City.

"On their arrival at York Point they found the middle of the street blocked with snow, a barricade which evidently had recently been shovelled there. When they attempted to force the horse through the snow barrier they were attacked by a gang of between thirty and forty hoodlums who were in the pay of the smugglers. Blocks of wood and other heavy missiles were hurled at the Customs men and three or four of the party were badly cut and bruised. But the nine Customs men not only succeeded in preventing the rescue of the smuggled liquor, but also managed to capture four or five of the gang's ringleaders."

While the above event was land-based similar events took place along the shore, frequently the smugglers' boats would be run aground on one of the many ledges and rocky protrusions ... although the smugglers tended to know the pitfalls better than their pursuers. Often on these occasions the booty would be buried either in the sand at the edge of the water or in caves or crannies in the cliffs. At other times either the Customs boats or the smugglers vessels would be wrecked and the cargo would sink to the bottom of the bay.

Little wonder then that the most frequent discovery of underwater treasure hunters is bottles of vintage wine and liquor!

During prohibition the Bay of Fundy was alive with fast boats carrying illegal cargo. These were the rum runners who obviously went to great lengths to avoid Indian Island and the Customs officers located there.

I remember hearing stories from the late Earl Tucker of L'Etete whose role in life was to catch said rum runners and bring them to justice on the Canadian side. Sadly enough I was too young or too stupid to take notes and only have vague memories of both hilarious and hair-raising tales as Earl steered his trusty launch back and forth across the bay, loud-hailing and frequently chasing the often faster boats intent on their illegal missions.

Prescott Dines, writing in the *St. Croix Courier* offers an all too brief account of the times.

"It was during the Depression that many Charlotte County fishermen reverted to rum running as a more lucrative living.

"In those days of Prohibition many fast boats from New York to Newfoundland endeavoured to run the gauntlet of customs and prevention officers –not always successfully. During this era one of the new Nova Scotia forty foot boats was fitted with three motors, gasoline, oil and a supply of food for three men.

"The father, son and one other crew member set out for St. Pierre (an island south of Newfoundland) but they encountered an August gale near Cape Breton. They disappeared altogether. The only evidence of their existence was the Captain's grain leather boots, washed ashore on the rocky coast of Cape Breton.

"Many successful trips from the mother ships to Maine, Massachusetts, Connecticut, Rhode Island and New York were accomplished 'by hook or crook,' I have even played golf in Florida with men from New York and Massachusetts who lived to tell of their many escapades during this adventurous era.

"Many of the trawl fishermen freely visited 'Rum Row' as it was called –vessels or mother ships anchored outside the three-mile limit of any Canadian land.

"The offshore trawlers would board these ships for free drinks –sometimes imbibing to excess. The result of this would be fish flying in all directions on board and finally a quiet sleep among the fish.

"Various boats and vessels found themselves ashore after the captains had visited 'Old John Barley Corn' too much and too often."

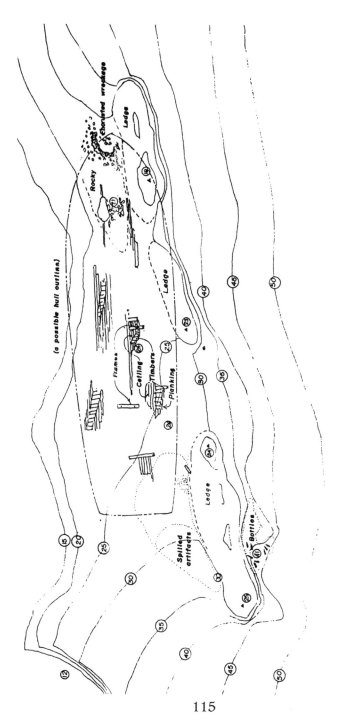

Wreck layout of British Ship *BRITANNIA* Wrecked Sandy Island, June 15, 1798

Scale 3m = 1 in.

New Brunswick Sea Stories

Questions of treasure hunting ... rights and ownership

In the course of my research I spent some time with Ken Keith, past president of the Underwater Archeological Society of New Brunswick, a man who firmly believes that those bottles divers are finding in shipwrecks should be left just where they are. And so should anything else related to the more than 1,900 shipwrecks that dot floors of the waters that surround three sides of the province of New Brunswick.

"Those items are important artifacts," Keith said. "If divers would let them stay right where they are then we would have almost a living history of our nautical past.

"Our underwater heritage is a non-renewable resource."

That heritage contains much of our history. The remains of the mast from the Marco Polo is still to be seen in the Gulf of St. Lawrence, off the coast of Prince Edward Island, just 300 meters off Cavendish Beach. A picture of the anchor said to be from the Marco Polo is believed to be decorating the garden of a wealthy Saint Johner's home.

"It's too bad it wasn't left on site for others to enjoy and examine. Perhaps the owner will decide someday to share it with the community. At least in a museum it would be a vivid reminder of a wonderful history and a wonderful ship."

Ken and some fellow members of the Underwater Archeological Society were invited to assist Parks Canada in doing the surveying of the wreck of the Marco Polo.

"We helped with the drawings and I helped Parks Canada put on a course on underwater archeology and preservation and conservation of underwater articles."

In fact Ken gets called on regularly to help teach such courses, a chore he relishes in the hope that the more underwater divers are educated in the archeological importance of ship wrecks the fewer problems there should be with people disturbing the site.

Seventeenth century fork found in Bay du Vin.

"The *Britannia*, a 932 ton British Navy ship hit a shoal and sank in 1798, just off Sandy Island in Head Harbour Passage and has been badly scavenged by amateur divers looking for souvenirs," Ken said.

A Dutch-built, three-masted square rigger, the *Britannia* was used to transport munitions and men between the United Kingdom and St. Andrews during the Napoleonic wars. The last time he checked there were still some canon balls, part of a hatch and at least one bottle left for history buffs to see.

He suggests that underwater photography is just as effective if someone wants to show off a 'find' and it doesn't disturb the site.

"Fortunately no one has yet found the *Plumper* We've looked for it and so have a lot of other people."

The *Plumper* would, without question, be a fascinating find for any underwater searcher. The British war ship went down on December 5, 1812. It was sailing from England to Saint John and was carrying enough gold to pay the English soldiers stationed in Saint John during the War of 1812. It

Anchor of the Marco Polo, said to be decorating the garden of a Saint John businessman.

struck a ledge between Chance Harbour and Dipper Harbour and was totally wrecked.

The exact amount of gold is not known, what is known is that fishermen of the area used to bring up silver dollars regularly from where the Plumper sank. The coins were discoloured with sea water but they would be cleaned up and put back into circulation where they were dubbed "Plumpers."

Ken explained that when a ship sinks the top is often beaten off by the waves and the sides break down flat and fill with sand. Once it is buried there is little exposure to oxygen and bacteria and it is somewhat preserved.

"It could last as long as 1,000 years as long as it's undisturbed. But once it is disturbed it deteriorates very rapidly. The sad part of it is that when people come in and disturb such a site they are exposing artifacts that don't mean a lot to most people but would be a major find for an archeologist."

There may be those who recognize the name Ladislav Malnor as that of the pilot who flew a Russian plane under the radar and landed it in Austria during the time of the Cold War in Europe. Today Ladislav lives in Miramichi City. He is still a professional pilot but he is also a professional diver and treasure hunter. His thoughts on underwater treasure hunting are diametrically opposed to those of Ken Keith.

"Yes, I dive in search of treasure. Right now I am fighting the government for my right to do so at the Oak Island site in Nova Scotia and I have petitioned the Queen to give me that right. I believe professional divers and treasure hunters play an important role. We are willing to work and take the risks involved to unearth often dangerous underwater sites in search of what treasures may be found there. More often than not our 'finds' end up in museums and collections where people can see them, instead of staying under the water to be appreciated by only a few select people."

Ladislav feels as strongly as Ken Keith about his convictions, which suggests it may be some time before a final ruling comes down on the sanctity of underwater treasure trove.

While diving near Bay du Vin Island, in the Miramichi area, Ladislav found a fork that he has had identified as of seventeenth century vintage. It was found in an area where he dives regularly. It was only uncovered because of the effect of the tides on the sandy bottom which on one day may cover wreckage then, on the following day, briefly uncover it for the lucky diver who happens to be there at the time.

Ladislav made his find after thoroughly researching the site in a library in Austria.

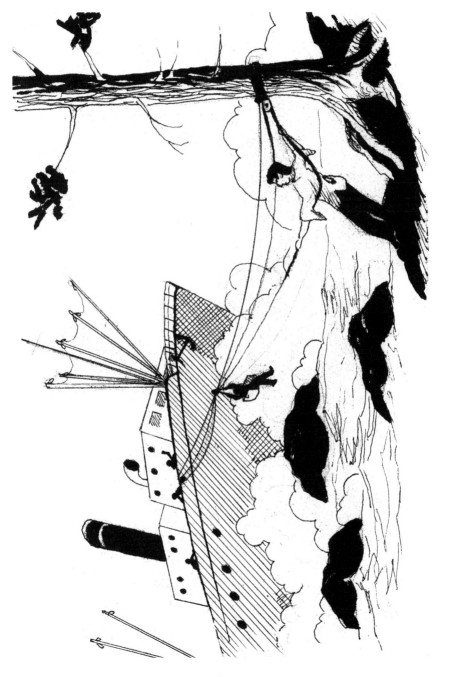

A Light Keeper's memories

In the course of my conversation with Ken Keith, about his underwater archeological experiences, he gave me a few pages of memoirs written, but to our knowledge not published, by Robert Splane. Dated April 5, 1977 they include anecdotes both from folklore and personal experience as remembered by him.

He provides a vivid story of the wreck, in 1935, of a Norwegian vessel carrying the interesting name of "The King's County."

"She went ashore on the halfway point or, as it was once called, 'Ferguson's Head.' She went ashore about two o'clock in the morning in a southeast rain storm. I remember the night well as I was working at Whistle House at Tiners Point and my shift was over at two o'clock. The Keeper, my brother, came on watch at two o'clock and heard several blasts of a steamer's whistle.

"The next day was Sunday and the shore and cliffs were lined with people who came to see and watch. Some of us fishermen who had boats row up from Sea View Beach and went aboard her and salvaged what we could. We didn't get very much of value, but we had a lot of fun.

"The only time we could get aboard her was when the

tide was down. I brought home a large, heavy hardwood table from the salon. I still have the table. I also got the watch bell, a bell used to ring the watches aboard ship. It has a lovely clear tone.

"Of course I got a lot of other things, such as canned fish and several bottles of very nice wine, a little whiskey and a few stone crocks of Hollands Gin, forty ouncers.

"The only things I have left are the table and the bell.

"*The Kings County* had a part load of grain and copper. The big storms that winter broke down her decks and her sides just folded in. By the next spring there was nothing left of her that could be seen."

"There were no lives lost. The youngest member of the crew swam ashore with a heaving line tied around his waist and when he made it to shore hauled a bigger line ashore to which they fastened a Bosun's Chair and the rest of the crew went ashore on it. She had a crew of thirty-three.

"I was told that when the young sailor who swam ashore with the heaving line went home to Norway he was given a big celebration and was given enough money to send him to college."

One of the stories that Splane wrote about was of a wreck that occurred in his grandfather's time. He remembers, as a boy of nine or ten, seeing the timbers of an old vessel sticking up out of the mud at Frenchman's Creek.

"My friends and neighbours, Howard and Russell Driscoll and I were fishing for trout at the lower end of Burchill's Brook which empties into Frenchman's Creek. I didn't know at the time what vessel it was but I was told in later years it was the last of the French pirate ship that was chased into Musquash Harbour by an English frigate.

"They had a battle in the harbour that lasted until the fog settled in but when the fog cleared the French pirate was no longer in Musquash Harbour. The English frigate, thinking that the French ship had sailed out in the fog set sail and went in search of her. But they never found her.

"What happened was that the French ship, sailing up along the harbour, noticed a break in the cliff and, it being high tide, sailed into an inlet. The ship ran aground in the mud and stayed there. That inlet has been known ever since as Frenchman's Creek.

"I was told by an old friend and neighbour that some of the men of the village of Irish Town would go there at night and dig for treasure but as far as I know none was found.

"I do have a souvenir of that battle between the English war ship and the French pirate. It is an iron ball, called a grape shot. It is nine inches in circumference and weighs about three pounds. My grandfather, John Splane, dug it out of what is known as Daley's Hill, the big steep hill going down to Black Beach.

"I remember being told as a boy that they dug out many of them but, as far as I know, the one that I have is the only one left from that battle in Musquash Harbour between the French Pirate and the English Frigate. I value it as a souvenir that has a link with the past of which my grandfather, John Splane, had a part."

New Brunswick Sea Stories

About the Author

Dorothy Dearborn began writing as a child and published her first poetry and short stories in the 1950s. A television career in the 1960s was interrupted by six years of front-line political involvement.

She worked as a reporter and served in various editorial positions, including that of city editor, at the Evening Times Globe and was editor of the weekly newspapers The Kings County Record and the Saint John Citizen.

Among her many interests are the promotion of adult literacy in New Brunswick and an often frustrating romance with Duplicate Bridge.

Mrs. Dearborn continues to work as a journalist. Her work may be found in numerous regional, national and international newspapers and magazines.

When not travelling the province researching and collecting stories and information for her work she can be found in front of her Macintosh computer at the family's 19th century farmhouse in Hampton, in the company of her ancient pony 'Soupy' and surrounded by a motley assortment of other critters.

She is married to Fred Dearborn, they have four grown children and numerous grandchildren.

About the Illustrator

Ralph Olive is a well-known Saint John artist who works primarily in watercolour. His work is shown regularly in regional galleries and is featured among a number of Canadian and American collections. Mr. Olive and Mrs. Dearborn share a common background as students and fellow graduates of Saint John High School.

New Brunswick Sea Stories